JIM BEARD'S

NEW

BARBECUE

COOKBOOK

 Random House, New York

All rights reserved under
International and Pan-American Copyright Conventions.
Published in New York by Random House, Inc.,
and in Toronto, Canada,
by Random House of Canada, Limited.

Library of Congress Catalog Card Number: 58-8761

Cover Ektachrome,
courtesy of United Fresh Fruit and Vegetable Association.
All pictures not otherwise credited
were taken by Von Miklos.

ACKNOWLEDGMENTS

We wish to thank the following for their help in the
production of this book: The Darien Provision Company,
Darien, Conn.; Allen Associates, New York, N. Y.;
Glass Institute, New York, N. Y.; Miss Virginia English,
Samuel Croot Co., Inc., New York, N. Y.

Manufactured in the United States of America.

FROM THE GRILL

THE FULL MEAL

FROM
THE
GRILL

Outdoor chefs can save a lot of wear and tear if they learn the basic

THE BASICS OF BARBECUING

What originated as a vogue for outdoor cookery is today an integral part of American family life. It is no longer a novelty to grill over charcoal or to roast on an electrically driven spit; it is part and parcel of our living pattern. In those parts of the country where indoor-outdoor living is not possible the year around, many designers and architects are creating charcoal units to go into their new houses.

This is an age of simplified living. It is also an age of simplified eating. Grilled and spitted roasted foods are delicious, nutritious and high in protein—attributes that are making them increasingly popular with a growing number of American families.

FIRE BUILDING

■ Charcoal cooking has achieved tremendous success, but many of its most ardent admirers wear themselves out before the meal trying to make a proper fire. This is basically a simple task, but a bit of study and practice is needed to get the hang of it.

Charcoal briquets are the most satisfactory and efficient type of fuel that I have found. You can buy other briquets of various substances, but they are not as satisfactory—in fact, some of them give off so much heat that they may damage expensive equipment. Wood charcoal is a good fuel but not as economical as charcoal briquets.

Briquets should be dry, so always keep them in a dry place. Damp or wet briquets not only create smoke but they take much longer to ignite and to build up to usable coals.

For kindling, the most satisfactory method is an odorless paint thinner or some other specially labeled fire starter. Build up 35 to 40 briquets, pyramid fashion, apply your paint thinner and wait 5 minutes before igniting. Briquets take about 30 minutes to get burning satisfactorily. One indication that they are burning properly will be the formation of a little white ash on your coals.

By all means, avoid making the fire too big—let the size of the food to be cooked determine the dimensions of the fire. Be sure to spread it evenly so that it extends just beyond the meat.

7

The number of briquets should depend on the size of your unit. A portable grill may take from 15 to 25 briquets, but a larger wheeled unit may require up to 45. Additional fuel may be added later, if needed.

The way to control the heat is to keep your fire level. Broiling temperature is always higher than that for roasting and should be around 350° at grill level. Varying temperatures are to be avoided. Sear the meat close to the coals but then keep it at a distance.

SEASONING

■ Outdoor cooks disagree as to when is the best time to salt the meat. My advice is not to salt it until it is almost done, as the salt may start the juices running too early in the cooking process.

Avoid unnecessary basting, particularly with highly seasoned sauces. The flavor of the meat will come through naturally if you baste it in its own juices while it is cooking.

BALANCING THE MEAT

■ Achieving the proper balance is the mark of the expert outdoor chef. If you watch an efficient operation you can't help but notice the care with which the veteran ties and trusses, always making certain that the meat is securely fixed. He will then pass the spit through the heaviest part, so that it is perfectly balanced, before he even applies his holding forks. If he fails to balance the meat properly, he will remove it from the spit and try again.

This is the only way to ensure the right balance, and knowing how to achieve it will double your proficiency at the grill.

Meat thermometers are invaluable

Abercrombie & Fitch Co.

AIDS TO BARBECUING

■ Certain necessities and a few luxuries are very pleasant to have. I don't believe in being the gadget type of outdoor cook, but I am exceedingly fond of good equipment. Among the necessities we will list:

1. Electric outlets near your cooking space. These are necessary for using electrically driven units and electric equipment which may be called auxiliary to the main units.

2. Asbestos gloves and leather or canvas work gloves should both be kept at the cooking site. Gloves are much better than tongs for handling charcoal. Asbestos gloves are invaluable for handling hot spits and pieces of equipment.

3. Foil has many uses in outdoor cooking. For instance, if you line the bottom of a portable grill or the fireplace of a large grill with several layers of heavy-duty aluminum foil, it will:

- Reflect back heat on the food and speed cooking.
- Cut down your consumption of briquets and help to make a more even temperature.
- Leave a clean firebox when you envelop the ashes, and catch any grease which has dripped through (and the foil can be easily disposed of in the trash can).

Furthermore, foil may be used to wrap meats, vegetables, game birds, fish, poultry and fruits—in short, anything that is to be cooked over charcoal or in the ashes. It is invaluable to the camper and the outdoor griller. It is also a perfect receptacle in which to carry any type of food to a picnic or camping site. It may be used as a container for freezing or for roasting or broiling.

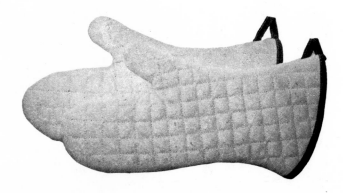

Keep asbestos gloves handy at the cooking site

Hammacher Schlemmer

4. I strongly urge the use of tongs rather than a fork when working at the grill. Tongs allow you to handle meat and vegetables without piercing them as the fork does. I cannot overemphasize the importance of having several heavy-duty units of this type.

5. Thermometers. Charcoal cookery has become so scientific that temperature is of major importance. A spit thermometer, with which some grills are now equipped, is invaluable. A grill thermometer is another piece of equipment that you will find useful at all times. The third adjunct is a meat thermometer, and for this I recommend one which has a dial that is marked from zero to 220°. I do not happen to agree with some of the temperatures recommended for meat by various authorities in this field, and I wouldn't be surprised if, after you start comparing, you disagreed, too.

6. I find that a bottle equipped with a sprinkler top, like the ones used to sprinkle clothes, is a necessity next to the grill when a bit of fat or oil drops into the firebox, causing a sudden conflagration.

You'll want more than one broiling basket

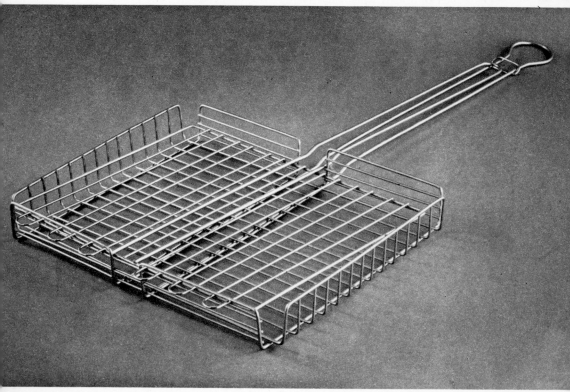

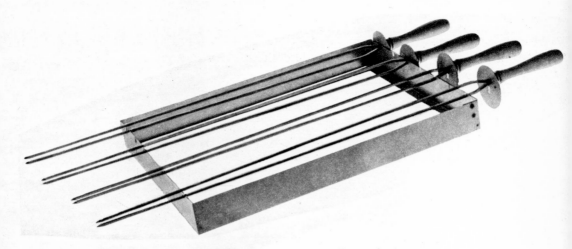

Skewers with wooden handles are best

A heavy-duty cutting board is essential

A big pepper mill and a big salt shaker are two absolute necessities

Abercrombie & Fitch Co.

7. Basters. I have seen Puerto Ricans and Mexicans use cornhusks for basting, and—much to my disgust—I've even seen string dish mops used. There are plenty of good basting brushes on the market, so just look around for one that performs the job efficiently.

8. Broiling baskets—holders. Hinged broilers and broiling baskets, including one with a small mesh for broiling small fish and meats, are useful to the active outdoor cook. Three or four of these should be in your prop box.

9. Many broilers and grills now come equipped with drip pans. These are helpful in preventing small conflagrations and they also catch some of the delicious juices that drip from roasts and grills.

10. Skewers. There is a tremendous variety of skewers on the market, but many of them are too long to be practical and others are much too frail. The ones with wooden handles are excellent. There is also an all-metal type that is quite short but exceedingly efficient. The very short ones are good for hors d'oeuvres as well as for roasts. For certain purposes bamboo chopsticks make handy tools, and long metal knitting needles are useful adjuncts when spitting small birds for the grill.

11. A heavy-duty cutting board and good knives are necessities for the outdoor griller. You will probably use your regular kitchen knives, but be sure they are good and sharp. There is no need for the fancy gadget type of outdoor knife sets.

12. A large pepper mill and a salt grinder or a very large shaker are absolute necessities.

13. Towels and pot holders are welcomed by most good cooks.

14. Other equipment includes skillets, big trays, cook-all baskets, serving spoons and various items which may be borrowed from your kitchen.

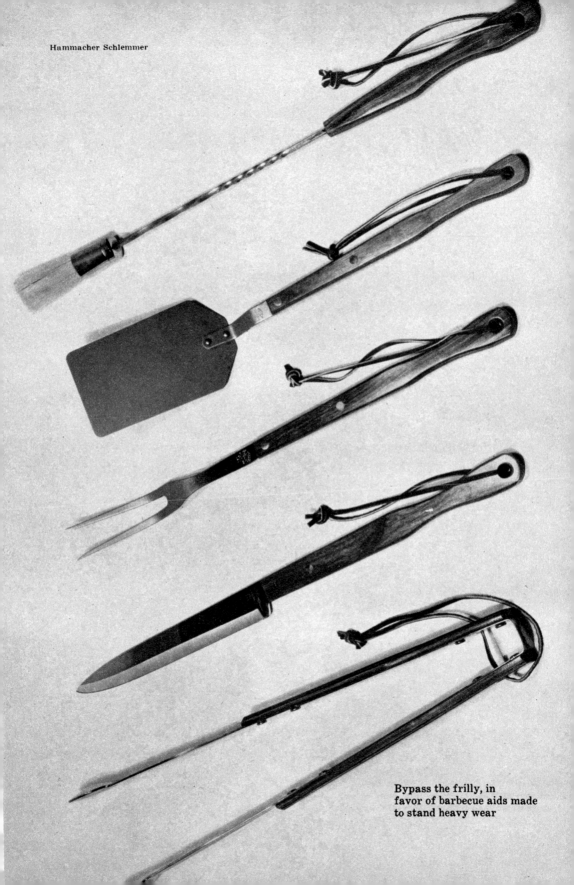

Hammacher Schlemmer

Bypass the frilly, in favor of barbecue aids made to stand heavy wear

There's more to broiling a steak than just slapping the meat on the

STEAKS

Beefsteak is probably the most popular meat in America, and certainly nothing is heartier or more satisfying than a good big steak, thick and juicy, and sizzling hot right from the grill.

TO BROIL A STEAK

■ Prepare the fire as recommended in Chapter 1. When it has become good white coals, and when your grill level registers about 350° to 370°, sear the steak on both sides to retain the juices throughout the grilling. Then lower the fire bed and continue cooking, turning over with the tongs until the proper degree of doneness is reached (see chart on page 25). To char it, bring the coals up to the meat and flame the steak before serving. Add salt and pepper just before the steak is done.

AMOUNTS TO BUY

■ Figure ¾ to 1 pound of steak per person. Have the steaks cut 1 to 3 inches thick, with excess fat removed. Frozen steaks may be cooked without thawing. Try not to choose a steak too large for your cooking facilities. You may find individual steaks the most satisfactory, particularly if you have a space problem.

THE BEST CUTS

■ Good beef is a cherry-red color when fresh and a purplish hue when well aged. The flesh of steaks should be well marbled with fat and edged with firm, flaky, cream-colored fat. The top grade is stamped U.S. Prime on the untrimmed cuts; the next best grade is stamped U.S. Choice. Some packers have their own names for various grades, such as Swift's Premium and Armour's Star.

You will find very good aged beef in some supermarkets. Order your extra-special steaks well in advance and get a properly aged one, which is tenderer than strictly fresh meat and has a slightly gamy flavor. The best steaks for grilling and broiling are these:

porterhouse

This has a cross-shaped bone in the middle, the fillet on one side of the bone and the contra-fillet on the other. It is probably the choicest cut of steak. For outdoor cooking, order it cut extra-thick—1½ to 3 inches.

t-bone

This is practically the same cut as porterhouse, except that it is further down the loin. It has less tenderloin than porterhouse.

sirloin

This is a fine cut from still lower down the loin. It is excellent eating and economical for a large group. Have it cut not less than 1½ inches thick. In England and France this cut is preferred for roasting, being considered far better than the rib cut generally used in this country.

rib steaks

These are called *entrecôte* by the French, and considered a delicacy. They are best when cut from the first three ribs. Have them cut with or without the bone, as you choose.

minute steaks

These are very thin steaks, cut from the rib, the sirloin or the shell. You will have better results if you pan-broil or sauté them quickly than if you grill them directly over the coals.

Also available are minute steaks which are cut thinner than usual. They are from ⅓ to 1 inch thick and may be cut from any of the parts of the loin we have mentioned. They generally provide 5 to 10 ounces of meat. Broil them quickly over a hot grill or saute them in butter in a hot skillet on the grill. They must be very rare to be worth eating.

VARIATION: Small individual minute steaks may be served on hot buns with a French sauce.

- Minute steaks may be cooked quickly and covered with rings of raw onions marinated in oil and vinegar.
- Cook minute steaks quickly and smother with sautéed mushrooms.

shell steaks

These are cut from the contra-fillet—the half of the porterhouse that is left when the fillet has been removed. They are the best choice if you want to serve individual steaks.

fillet

This is really the tenderest part of the tenderloin. If you are serving several people, it is best to buy the whole tenderloin and either cut it

Flank steak, red-rare and sliced on the diagonal, is delicious

yourself into individual steaks or cook it whole. Or you can cut part of it into steaks and spit and roast the rest. You will find it cheaper per pound when you buy it in a whole piece.

flank steak

This is a triangular piece of meat which many people feel is not suitable for grilling. If properly grilled and carved, however, it is one of the most luscious bits of beef that can be had.

Flank steak, cooked just to the rare stage and carved in thin slices on the diagonal, is excellent eating. Have the butcher trim the steak well. Broil it quickly, allowing 3 to 4 minutes to a side, until it is nicely charred on the outside and still juicy red in the middle. Season to taste with salt and pepper and cut it on the diagonal, holding the knife so that it slopes from left to right.

VARIATION: Oriental. Marinate the steak in ½ cup of sherry, ½ cup of soy sauce, 2 chopped cloves of garlic and ¼ cup of chopped fresh ginger or 1 teaspoon of ground ginger. Soak it for several hours, turning frequently. Broil and carve as above.

VARIATION: Chili-Oriental. Add 1 tablespoon of chili powder to the above marinade.

17

OTHER CUTS

■ Some of the less expensive grades of steak, such as top round and rump, as well as short ribs, may be broiled if they are first marinated.

To cook chunks of beef on skewers, the best choice is sirloin, though the cheaper cuts may be used if marinated to make them tender. Buy beef for this purpose by the piece and cut it into cubes yourself.

marinated steak

You can broil the less tender cuts, such as top round, with delicious results by first marinating the meat. Mix 1 cup of olive oil, juice of 1 lemon, 1 crushed clove of garlic, a dash of salt and 1 teaspoon of freshly ground black pepper. Pour this over the steak, turn several times to be sure it is evenly coated, and let stand in a warm place for several hours or overnight. Grill as usual, omitting seasoning.

STEAK SPECIALTIES

barbecued steak

Make a paste of 2 to 3 teaspoons of dry mustard, salt to taste and enough bourbon or other whisky to moisten. Spread this on the steak and let it stand for ½ hour. Broil as usual.

steak rosemary

Cover both sides of the steak with rosemary pressed in with the heel of your hand. (Spice Islands is an excellent brand of dried herbs.) Grill as usual and season just before serving. Add a good pat of butter.

pepper steak

Use cracked Spice Island pepper, or crush your own from whole peppercorns with a rolling pin or mortar and pestle. Press the pepper into the steak on both sides. Let it stand for an hour. Grill as usual, salting as you turn the steak. When done, flame with ¼ cup of cognac.

churrasco

This South American version of beefsteak is wonderfully good eating. For 6 persons, buy a large sirloin of 7 pounds or more, about 3 inches thick. Or you can use 2 steaks with a combined weight of 7 or more pounds. Broil the steak according to previous instructions and during the cooking baste once or twice with butter seasoned to taste with dried rosemary. Cook the meat just to the rare state and char it at the last minute.

Meanwhile prepare the following sauce: Sauté 2 cups of finely chopped green onion in ½ pound of butter until just soft. Add a dash or two of dried rosemary, 1½ teaspoons of salt, 1 tablespoon of freshly ground black pepper, 1 cup of white wine and ½ cup of wine vinegar. Bring this to a boil, lower the heat and simmer for 5 minutes. Taste for seasoning and add another large lump of butter.

When the steak is ready, cut it in rather thin diagonal slices and put them in the sauce for a minute. Serve each person some of the sauce with the meat. Good accompaniments for this dish are home-fried potatoes, sautéed or roasted onions and French bread with butter.

VARIATION: Subsitute any other steak cut or a slice of rare rib roast of beef and serve it in the same manner.

beefsteak jérome le plat

In spite of the French name, this dish was originally Italian. The secret is in the sauce.

Prepare your favorite hollandaise sauce and when it is thickened add the juice of 1 lemon, 2 tablespoons of tomato purée, 1 teaspoon of freshly ground black pepper and a touch of Worcestershire. Just before serving add ¼ cup of finely chopped parsley. (These amounts are for 1 cup of hollandaise.)

Broil the steak in your favorite manner, slice it diagonally and bathe the slices in the sauce.

beefsteak pizzaioula

This is another Italian version of steak, popular with those who like the flavor of tomatoes.

Grill 2-inch sirloin steak or *entrecôte* for 4 persons according to instructions. Meanwhile prepare the following sauce: Sauté 4 chopped cloves of garlic in ¼ cup of olive oil. Add 1 large tin of Italian tomatoes (those canned with basil) and cook this down to half the original amount. Season to taste with salt, fresh black pepper and 1 teaspoon of oregano.

When the steak is done to your satisfaction, remove it to a hot platter, pour the sauce over it and top with finely chopped Italian parsley and sautéed mushrooms.

filet mignon with tarragon butter

Figure on 2 small *filets mignons* per person. They should be about 1 inch thick. Brush them well with oil and broil to a rare stage over charcoal. Remove to a hot platter or board and top each with tarragon butter, which is made by creaming ¼ pound of butter with 1 teaspoon of dry mustard, 1½ teaspoons of tarragon and a dash of fresh black pepper.

19

Tabasco

roquefort broiled steak

Crush a large clove of garlic with a heavy fork in a small bowl. Add ½ pound of Roquefort cheese and 4 tablespoons of softened butter. Cream together well and flavor with 2 teaspoons of dry mustard and a dash of Worcestershire sauce. Grill your steak as usual. When you are turning it, spread the browned side with the cheese mixture, which should melt into a most pleasing sauce for the steak when it is done.

sliced larded fillet on french bread

For hearty appetites allow 1 pound of fillet for each guest. Be sure to get whole, not sliced, fillet. Ask the butcher to lard the fillets for you (if you have a larding needle you can do it yourself). For each fillet, soak 3 thin strips of salt pork in cognac for 2 hours. Run them through the edges of the beef with the larding needle.

Roll the fillets in coarsely crushed black pepper and broil over coals for about 25 minutes, to 120° on thermometer, turning often. Season to taste with salt. Or you can spit them and roast over charcoal for the same length of time. If you use a meat thermometer, remove the fillets at 120°. They will be very rare—the way they taste best.

To serve: Cream ½ pound of butter and blend it with 1½ to 2 teaspoons of rosemary. Heat French bread and split the loaf. Spread each half liberally with the rosemary butter. Cut the fillet into paper-thin slices and arrange them on the hot buttered French bread. Guests can eat them as sandwiches or with knife and fork.

chateaubriand marchand de vin

A Châteaubriand is the most luxurious cut from the center part of the fillet. It should be very thick and weigh from 1 to 2 pounds. Buy marrow bones and have the butcher cut them so that the marrow can be extracted in one piece.

Broil the Châteaubriands. During the cooking, brush them frequently with melted butter and turn them often. Meanwhile, extract the marrow and slice it in thin rounds. Poach the marrow rounds for about 1 minute in boiling salted water.

Prepare the following sauce (since a Châteaubriand has no fat, it is at its best only when served with a sauce): Sauté ⅔ cup of finely chopped green onions in ¼ pound of butter until just colored. Add 1 cup of red wine (preferably a good Bordeaux) and cook this down to half its volume. Add 1 can of brown gravy, a dash of cognac, a large pat of butter and the juice of a lemon. Sprinkle the sauce heavily with chopped parsley.

When the meat is done to your satisfaction, remove it to hot plates, pour the sauce over each portion and top with slices of poached marrow.

lamb steak

There is a great difference between real spring lamb and yearling lamb. The latter more nearly resembles good mutton. True spring lamb is hard to find. Check with your butcher and see what he can do for you.

Lamb steak is cut from the leg. It should be about 1 inch thick. If good mutton is available in your neighborhood, it's even better for steak. Grill slowly, turning often, and season to taste just before serving. Be sure to serve it on piping-hot plates. If you like the flavor of tarragon, sprinkle a little on the steaks as they grill. Or press rosemary into both sides of the steak and grill.

For lamb steaks, you may have to buy a whole leg of lamb and ask your butcher to cut you some slices off the meaty end. (You can use the shank end to braise with lentils for another meal.) You should get 4 to 5 good-sized steaks from the average leg. If this seems too extravagant, have a shoulder of lamb boned and rolled and then cut into slices for steaks.

Mutton may be treated in the same way, but be sure to cut away the excess fat that comes on it.

lamb in curry marinade
Crush a clove of garlic, add 1 tablespoon of curry powder, a bit of ginger and ¾ cup of soy sauce. Marinate the steaks in this for 1 hour before grilling.

ham steak
I feel that good ham steak should be from 1½ to 2½ inches thick for grilling over the coals. It should be grilled slowly over a low heat so that it cooks without charring too much. Its own fat will provide the crispy outside that it needs to be delicious. A ham steak between 1½

Broiled whole, tenderloin makes excellent steak sandwiches, especially when

and 2½ inches will need between 40 and 60 minutes of grill time to make it thoroughly tender and well cooked.

VARIATION: When the ham steak is ¾ cooked, combine with a mixture of ½ cup of honey, the juice of 1 lemon and 2 teaspoons (more or less) of dry mustard.

VARIATION: Marinate the ham steak in enough pineapple juice to cover. Add ¼ cup of sherry, 1 teaspoon of dry mustard and a few dashes of Worcestershire sauce. Baste the ham steak with the marinade several times during the cooking.

steak sandwiches

You may use any large steak, cut thick, for steak sandwiches. Grill it as you normally would, and when it is done, cut it in thin slices and serve between pieces of warmed or toasted French bread well buttered.

An excellent way to make steak sandwiches for a crowd is to buy a whole tenderloin. Tell your butcher you're going to cook it whole and have him trim it for you. Oil it or grease it well with butter, place it on a grill over hot coals. Turn it often and baste constantly with additional fat, for the tenderloin is a very lean cut. Depending on its thickness, a tenderloin will take from 10 to 20 minutes to cook to a delicious rare state. Season it before or during cooking and serve in thin slices, on French bread as above.

served in thin slices on French bread with onions and mustard

pork steak

The French do this to perfection, although it is a much neglected dish in this country. The steaks are cut from the fresh ham, as it is called in the East, or the leg, as it is called in the West—and should be between 1½ and 2 inches thick. Pork steak must be cooked slowly and well. Rub it with a little butter or melted pork fat before placing it on a grill over a fairly slow fire. Turn it over and cook until it is nicely browned, tender and cooked through. Salt and pepper it well and serve with a devil sauce (see the chapter on sauces and marinades).

GRILLING WITH PROPANE

■ If you buy one of the ceramic grills using propane fuel (see Equipment, page 122), you'll find that the technique for grilling a thick steak in this manner is different. Consult the manufacturer's handbook for the exact timing. The secret of successful grilling on this type of unit is to sear close to the flame. Envelop the steak in aluminum foil and finish the cookery on a higher notch away from the intense heat which the gas and ceramic tile give off. The results are practically the same as those obtained with charcoal.

When grilling over propane, first sear the meat, then salt it

Foil-wrap the meat and complete the cooking. Unwrap and serve

STEAK TIMETABLE

1 **INCH**	Very rare—8 minutes Rare—9 minutes Medium—12 minutes Well done—15-18 minutes
1½ **INCHES**	Very rare—8-10 minutes Rare—10-12 minutes Medium—13-15 minutes Well done—15-20 minutes
2 **INCHES**	Very rare—14-18 minutes Rare—18-25 minutes Medium—25-32 minutes Well done—30-45 minutes
2½ **INCHES**	Very rare—20-27 minutes Rare—25-35 minutes Medium—35-40 minutes Well done—45-60 minutes or more
3 **INCHES** **OR** **MORE**	Should be cooked with a meat thermometer inserted in the thickest part. Use the following temperature table: Very rare—120°-130° Rare—125°-135° Medium—145°-155° Well done—160°-170°

● The only way to make absolutely certain that a steak is cooked the way you want it is to use the age-old knife test. With a sharp knife cut a small incision in the flesh next to the bone and see how red it is. Warning: If night has fallen, use a good flashlight to check the color.

Absolutely essential items in any barbecue chef's bag of tricks, these

HAMBURGERS & FRANKFURTERS

General Foods

Once upon a time, before the Pizza Age, hamburgers and frankfurters were the most popular foods in the country. There are few things better than hamburger, if it is seasoned properly, cooked just right and served up hot and rare.

I am old-fashioned. I still like frankfurters with skin, and hunt them down ferociously. Hot dogs are also indispensable to the outdoor grill—in fact, you couldn't maintain one without them.

HAMBURGERS

plain hamburgers

Buy lean ground beef with no more than 25 to 30 per cent fat and allow at least ½ pound per person. If you are serving hamburgers on buns, make two patties of ¼ pound each per person. The less you handle the raw meat, the juicier the cooked hamburger will be, so form the patties gently, with a light touch. Shape the hamburgers around a cube of ice to ensure a juicy, fresh patty. Brush with melted butter or oil. Sear them well on both sides and then continue grilling, turning often, until they are done as you like them. Personally, I feel they should be crusty brown on the outside but still juicy and rare in the middle. Season with salt and pepper as you turn.

Serve on hot toasted buns or hot toasted French bread with a choice of good relishes and pickles. Don't forget the mustard (a sharp English type or one of the excellent French imports) and freshly grated horse-radish for people who prefer something sharper than the customary pickle condiments.

cheese hamburgers

To each pound of ground beef add ½ cup of grated sharp Cheddar cheese, 1 tablespoon of Worcestershire sauce and 1 grated onion. Season to taste with freshly ground pepper and form into cakes. Wrap each cake with a slice of bacon and grill as above. These are exceptionally good served with sliced raw onion marinated in an olive-oil and wine-vinegar dressing and plenty of hot mustard.

savory hamburgers

To each pound of ground beef add 1 medium onion chopped very fine, ½ cup of chopped ripe olives and 1 tablespoon of Spice Islands mushroom powder. Grill as above, seasoning to taste with salt and pepper as the meat cooks. Serve these hamburgers with crisp fried potatoes and a salad of sliced tomatoes dressed with olive oil and wine vinegar and garnished with black olives and strips of anchovies.

beefsteak bismarck

For 4 persons, mix together 2 pounds of ground beef, 2 tablespoons of melted butter, ¼ cup of finely chopped green onions, 1 teaspoon of salt and 2 teaspoons of fresh black pepper. Form into 4 cakes and broil.

Serve each hamburger cake topped with a hot soft-fried egg. For accompaniments have plain boiled potatoes liberally dressed with butter and chopped parsley, tomatoes broiled with a seasoning of chopped garlic and basil, and plenty of cold ale.

herbed hamburgers

To 1 pound of hamburger add ¼ cup each of chopped chives and parsley, 2 teaspoons of dried rosemary, 1 egg, salt and freshly ground black pepper. Mix well and form into cakes. Cook as above.

mexican hamburgers

To 1 pound of hamburger add 1 small green pepper and 1 onion, both chopped, 1 tablespoon of chili powder, 1 tablespoon of chili sauce, and salt and pepper to taste. Mix well, form into cakes and cook just as you did the herbed hamburgers.

VARIATION: Serve plain hamburgers covered with chili con carne. If you like them very sharp, spike the chili with a dash of Tabasco.

hamburger and eggplant

Allow 2 rather thin slices of eggplant for each serving. Dredge them in seasoned flour and grill lightly, just until they are brown and tender. Keep them hot. To 1 pound of hamburger add 1 small onion grated and 1 smallish clove of garlic grated. Season to taste with salt and freshly ground black pepper. Form into patties about the size of the eggplant slices and fairly thin—½ to ¾ of an inch thick. Grill quickly. Serve each hamburger patty sandwiched between two eggplant slices, with your favorite barbecue or tomato sauce poured over each serving.

corned beefburgers

Here's a tasty change from the usual hamburger fare. Use a good brand of canned corned-beef hash or—much better—make your own mixture. To 4 cups of chopped corned beef add 2 cups of cubed, lightly boiled potatoes, freshly ground black pepper to taste, 1 or 2 onions chopped, and a pinch of nutmeg. Mix well and form into patties. Brush with melted butter and grill over hot coals or in a hot skillet. Cook slowly until the patties are crusty and brown on the outside. Serve with poached eggs and a tart sauce, such as a chili sauce.

VARIATION: To the corned-beef mixture add 4 tablespoons of chili sauce and 1 green pepper chopped very fine.

hamburger rarebit

Cover hamburger patties with your favorite welsh-rarebit recipe, which may be prepared in the electric skillet beside your grill.

First, place an ice cube in each raw hamburger

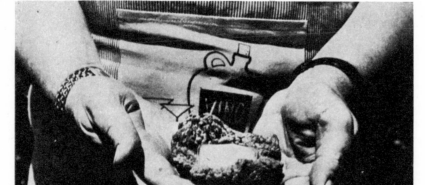

The grilling melts the ice and leaves the meat juicy

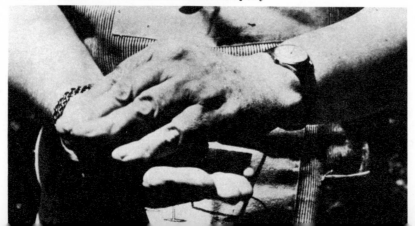

FRANKFURTERS

■ Most Americans think they know all there is to know about cooking frankfurters. They simply grill them in a pan or folding grill (or, heaven forbid, boil them), slap them on a tasteless frankfurter roll, pass the mustard and piccalilli, and that's it. Actually the lowly hot dog is a very versatile animal if properly treated and can be distinctive eating.

30

First of all, if you're going to serve them sandwich fashion, don't feel bound to use the standard frankfurter roll. Try instead some tender little finger rolls from your local bakery or, better yet, some small French rolls. You'll find either of these finer in texture and better flavored than the mass-produced standby.

Try some of the following suggestions for sprucing up the hot dog:

1. Cut a deep slit in one side of each frankfurter, insert some sharp Cheddar cheese and wrap the frankfurter with a strip of bacon to hold it together. Fasten with a toothpick, and grill.

2. Grill whole frankfurters and serve with home-made chili.

3. Pan-grill thick slices of beefsteak tomatoes, grill frankfurters and serve each one on top of a tomato slice.

4. Heat frankfurters or knockwurst over hot coals. Cut them into bite-size pieces, insert a toothpick in each one, and serve with a large bowl of hot barbecue sauce for guests to dunk their portions into. This is good as a hot snack with drinks.

5. For 6 people, take 12 large frankfurters or 6 knockwurst and slice them down the middle. Mash ½ pound of liverwurst and combine with 2 tablespoons of grated onion, ½ cup of sour cream and a dash of Tabasco. Stuff the frankfurters or knockwurst with this mixture, brush with mustard and roll each two in foil. Cook in the foil on the grill for 12 to 15 minutes, turning them twice during the process.

6. Grill frankfurters, place on toasted rolls, top with pickle relish and a slice of cheese. Reheat to melt the cheese.

7. Texas hots: Serve grilled franks on toasted rolls and heap ground meat and chili and chopped raw onion in the sandwich.

8. Put grilled franks in hot toasted buttered rolls, add some good barbecue sauce and heat.

9. Top frankfurter sandwiches with the following sauce: Sauté chopped onion in butter until just soft, add tomato sauce, season to taste with salt and pepper, bring to a bubbling boil. Add sour cream to taste, cook until just hot but not boiling.

10. French fashion: Spread a French roll with garlic butter to which you have added some chopped chives and parsley, add a grilled frankfurter and a slice of cheese. Wrap the whole thing in a piece of foil and heat until the cheese melts. Have a bowl of hot barbecue sauce for everyone to dunk his serving in.

11. Long frankfurter roll: Split a loaf of French bread the long way, butter it with garlic butter and toast lightly. On the bottom half arrange sliced tomatoes, sliced onions, sliced cucumbers, frankfurters or knockwurst which have been split and grilled, and mayonnaise. Add cheese if you like. Top with the other half of the loaf. Cut through in thick slices the round way. Serve with radishes and green onions.

Barbecued chops of lamb, mutton, pork and veal appeal to everyone,

CHOPS

even the calorie counters, if they are grilled with care and patience

T here is something palate-teasing about the word "chops." Chops are exciting to the nostrils when they are cooking. They are delicately tempting to look at and they are excellent food for the person who needs to watch his diet. They take patience and must be treated carefully on a grill; for while some chops are delicious when pink and rare, most of them require a great deal more cooking and attention than do steaks. For cooking chops on a propane-gas grill, I suggest that you consult the book which accompanies the grill.

LAMB CHOPS

■ Lamb chops are no good at all if they are not cut thick, and by thick I mean anywhere from 1½ to 3 inches in thickness. Lamb chops should be of U.S. Prime or U.S. Choice meat. If you are going to grill the chops, don't try to take economical short cuts. I think a loin chop is the only cut for the outdoor grill. Rib chops are just a little delicate for this type of treatment unless a rack of 3 or 4 small chops is cooked for each person. This, of course, means extra work.

broiled lamb chops

To be perfectly cooked, a loin lamb chop should be well browned and crispy on the outside. The fat should be crisp and well done and the center should be pink in color. Start the chops over a medium low fire and turn them once or twice. Test them for doneness by slitting the meat close to the bone to see the degree of pinkness they have reached. Just as with steak, if you want them very charred, you may bring up the heat for the last few moments. A 2- to 2½-inch lamb chop should take about 12 to 14 minutes to broil and still be pink.

VARIATION: Tarragon Chops. Cream together ¼ cup butter and 2 teaspoons dried tarragon which has been soaked for 30 minutes in 2 tablespoons of white wine or vermouth. Make small incisions in the fat side of the lamb chops with a sharp knife and stuff bits of the tarragon butter in each chop. Broil and brush with remaining tarragon butter before serving.

33

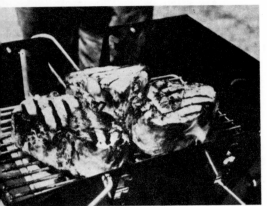

Lamb chops should be cut thick. Broil them until they're crisp outside, rare inside

- Lamb chops stuffed with mushrooms. Chop ½ pound of mushrooms very fine, sauté in 6 tablespoons butter for 30 minutes over low heat. Salt and pepper to taste, and just before removing from fire stir in 1 teaspoon flour and allow it to cook until slightly thickened. Cut a pocket in four 2-inch loin lamb chops and stuff with the mushroom mixture. Secure the chops with small skewers, either wood or metal. Broil the chops as directly above.
- Lamb Chops with Garlic. Lamb and garlic have always had an affinity for each other. Crush and finely chop or press 2 cloves garlic for 6 chops. Combine the chopped garlic with 3 tablespoons olive oil and 2 teaspoons chopped parsley. Split the chops and add a spoonful of this mixture to each pocket. These do not have to be skewered. Broil the chops according to directions above and brush with additional garlic. Butter before serving.

saddle lamb chops

For centuries the English have been cutting thick lamb chops right across the saddle, thus giving each person two loin chops joined together. These should be cut about 2 inches thick; and if you wish, a kidney may be rolled into the side of each one, although it is my belief that the kidney cooks too much when prepared this way. Tie a strip of rather lean bacon around each chop and broil slowly. Saddle lamb chops are wonderfully good served with potatoes baked in the ashes and accompanied by an excellent cole slaw.

ACCOMPANIMENTS: Lamb chops are delicious served with crisp sautéed potatoes and unadorned water cress. They are so good themselves that they need no saucing.

MUTTON CHOPS

■ Mutton is a word that is almost taboo in America; yet I am certain if you find good American or Canadian mutton, have the chops cut thick and grill them properly, you will be delighted with the results. Broiled mutton chops, to be at their best, should be cut very thick. If you like the taste of garlic, rub well with a bud and grill them over a fairly slow to medium heat. During part of the procedure I always turn them on the fat side so that the large amount of fat, which is normal in good mutton, has a chance to dry out. Mutton must be served on very hot plates or the fat will congeal and make a most unattractive service.

english mutton chops

Like the English cut of lamb chop, these are usually cut across the saddle. However, one New York restaurant which is famous for its mutton chops cuts them from the rack, about three ribs to a chop. In either case the chops should be grilled on three sides and should be served according to your preferred state of doneness. I feel that cole slaw and baked potatoes are a must, as well as good ale or beer.

PORK CHOPS

■ There is one thing to remember when cooking pork: it must be well done. Cook it slowly, a good distance from the coals, and turn it often. It should be thoroughly cooked.

Buy thick chops from the loin—about 1½ inches thick—and allow 2 chops per person. Cook them slowly, turning often, and season to taste with salt and pepper as they cook. Gash the fat before placing the chops on the grill; this helps to melt it down.

country-style pork chops

Cover pork chops (2 to a person) with milk and coarsely ground black pepper. Let them marinate in this mixture for several hours. Remove and grill the chops slowly over a medium fire, turning often and allowing the chops to cook for some time on the fat side. Salt them just before serving. Serve with a real old-fashioned cream gravy made with the milk in which you marinated the chops. I like to serve home-fried potatoes and broiled apple rings, which should be sprinkled with granulated sugar for the last few minutes of their grilling.

deviled pork chops

Grill thick loin chops according to directions given above. When they are cooked through and nicely browned, remove each chop and press into buttered crumbs. Return to grill to brown the crumbs. Each chop should

Veal chops can be rather disappointing when cooked over charcoal, but they

have one surface nicely coated with browned crumbs. Serve with a deviled sauce (see "Sauces and Marinades").

italian-style pork chops

Have the chops cut about 2½ inches thick and allow 1 large chop per person. Cut a pocket in each chop. Combine 3 cloves of finely chopped garlic, 1 tablespoon of chopped fresh basil leaves or 1½ teaspoons of dried sweet basil, ½ teaspoon of salt, ½ cup of chopped mushrooms and ¼ cup of tomato purée. Blend; add a spoonful of this mixture to the pocket in each chop. Grill slowly, basting with a little garlic-flavored olive oil from time to time, and serve with buttered noodles topped with Parmesan cheese. You may make additional sauce and cook it for 15 minutes to pour over the cooked chops if you wish.

pork chops in ceramic grill

A ceramic grill is ideal for cooking pork chops, because they are crisply seared and finished off in foil on the grill. The natural juices are maintained and the chops are delicately tender.

VEAL CHOPS

■ Veal chops are the least desirable for a charcoal grill. They are, however, sensationally good when seasoned and grilled in foil on a ceramic grill. They should be cut 1½ to 2 inches thick and should be bordered

turn out fine if you season them, wrap them in foil and broil over propane gas

with a strip of bacon. Grill them slowly and baste from time to time with bacon fat or butter. Salt and pepper to taste.

stuffed veal chops

Have the chops cut 2 to 2½ inches thick from the loin. Cut a pocket in each chop. For 6 large chops, cream together ¼ pound of butter, 1 teaspoon of chopped chives, 1 tablespoon of finely chopped parsley, 1 tablespoon of chopped tarragon or 1 teaspoon of dried tarragon. Stuff the pocket with this herbed butter and secure with a skewer which will hold the barding bacon as well. (Barding means to wrap or cover the surface of a bird or meat with thin slices of fat, usually salt pork. This is tied around the meat during part of the cooking process.) Broil slowly, brushing with bacon fat or butter. Salt and pepper to taste.

farm-style veal chops

Soak thick veal chops in enough milk to cover. Add 1 large onion thinly sliced. When the chops have marinated for 3 to 4 hours, remove and grill over medium coals, turning repeatedly and brushing with melted butter. Make an old-fashioned cream gravy with the milk in which the chops were soaked. Sauté the onion rings in butter until they are soft and lightly browned and add 2 tablespoons of flour. When this is well blended and lightly browned, gradually stir in the milk and continue stirring until it thickens. Season to taste with salt and freshly ground black pepper. Serve with tiny new potatoes boiled in their jackets.

For centuries, people have roasted meat on spits. Modern equipment

ROASTS

makes the job fun—and ensures a tender, juicy main course as well

Many people consider spitting the only true form of roasting. It is the oldest, although our ancestors, unfortunately, knew nothing of electrically driven spits. We know that the juiciness and evenness of cooking are two of the results most desired from good spit roasting. The flavor imparted by charcoal or wood smoke is one of America's most sought-after gustatory experiences, and any barbecue enthusiast who denies himself the pleasure of spit-roasted meats—especially in these days of easy-to-run attachments—is missing at least half the fun of barbecue cookery.

PREPARING ROASTS FOR THE GRILL

■ There are certain rules which must be followed if one is going to use modern equipment successfully. Meat must be correctly trussed, tied and balanced on the spit. If the meat is off center, you stand in danger of ruining your motor and stopping the spit. Furthermore, the meat will be spottily cooked. The meat should not slip around on the spit. The holding forks and, if necessary, additional skewers should be used to ensure its holding firm during the cooking process. Certain meats will shift position while roasting because the fat renders, causing the weight to shift. That is why better grills are equipped with compensators with which to adjust the spit balance during the roasting period.

ROASTING TEMPERATURES

■ Roasting temperatures for meat should be about the same as for broiling, if not just a little lower. Additional briquets or pieces of charcoal may be added during the roasting process to obtain a steady temperature on the spit surface. The average spit temperature for roasting is around 300°. Spits should turn away from the cook, thus enabling the fat to drip on the upward motion of the spit into the dripping pan. The Bartron unit is equipped with a special firebox for spitting; but if you do not have such a unit, build your fire toward the back of your grill and put a dripping pan or foil in front of it.

GENERAL RULES FOR ROASTING

■ Cooking time varies a great deal according to wind, outside temperature, quality of meat and evenness of cooking temperature. Therefore, I feel it is exceedingly important to use a meat thermometer for good results. Remember that meat continues cooking *after* it is removed from the spit for as much as 30 minutes. As a consequence, when I give a cooked temperature, the meat should be removed at that moment and coasted (held) for 15 to 20 minutes before carving. This gives the juices a chance to set and makes the roast more flavorful and delicious.

If your spit is properly balanced and turns evenly, basting is not necessary. If, however, you wish to impart another flavor or coating to the meat, you'll have to baste it. Too, if the meat is extremely lean, it needs the lubrication that only a good baste can give it.

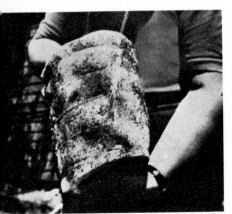 

Spit a standing rib roast diagonally in order to achieve perfect balance

BEEF

standing rib roast

This roast has achieved the greatest popularity of any joint. Roasts of from 2 to 7 ribs may be cooked with ease, for your spit will accommodate them. Have the butcher cut them short—a 7-inch cut is very good. Ask him to remove the chine bone and tie the roast securely. For best results, standing ribs should be spitted on the diagonal and balanced perfectly. Force the spit into the cut side of the meat and diagonally through the length of the roast. (If the meat is not properly balanced on the spit, it will rotate unevenly. Therefore, you must experiment and

40

possibly re-spit the roast several times to achieve perfect balance. Some spits are equipped with a counterweight system that aids in this procedure.) Tighten the screws of the holding forks. Insert your meat thermometer so that it does not touch a bone and roast over a medium fire until the thermometer reads 125° (very rare). Coast (hold) on spit or remove from the grill and allow it to stand in a warm place for 15 to 20 minutes before removing the spit and carving. It will take a 5-rib roast, which is my favorite, around 2½ hours to achieve the inner temperature of 125°. A 2-rib roast is ideal for small family groups and usually takes just over an hour to be perfectly rare.

rolled rib roasts

Rolled rib roasts have never been a favorite of mine. Many people prefer them, feeling that they are more easily spitted, although they should also be done on the diagonal. Cooking time is about the same as for a standing rib and the roast should be removed from the heat when it reaches an internal temperature of 125°. Baste with beef drippings.

spencer roast

This is a cut more frequently used on the West Coast than on the East Coast. It is a rib roast with the bone and a good deal of the fat removed. A Spencer may be spitted straight through the roast, or you may spit it as you do a standing rib. It is ideal for roast-beef sandwiches. Roast the Spencer to an internal temperature of 125° if you want it rare.

sirloin roast

This is England's favorite joint for roasting and is occasionally used over here. Known in the eastern part of the country as a boneless strip, it is spitted and roasted like the Spencer and makes delicious eating.

rump roast

If your butcher carries U.S. Prime beef, a rolled, barded and tied rump roast is a very tasty change. Balance it well on the spit—not an easy job because its shape is apt to vary a good deal—and cook to an internal temperature of 125°.

whole roast tenderloin

A whole tenderloin done on a spit makes a simple and elegant dish, and in spite of the cost per pound at the butcher's, it is really economical, as I pointed out earlier, because it's all solid meat. Have the butcher roll it in a thin sheet of pounded suet and tie it securely. Salt and freshly ground pepper are all this delicious morsel needs, although I sometimes like to sprinkle it with a little rosemary or rosemary seasoning powder as well. Spit it through the center and roast it about 35 minutes, or until it is nicely crisp on the outside but still rare in the center. It is impossible to give exact cooking time because each cooking unit tends to work a little differently from others. When it is done to your satisfaction, remove the tenderloin from the spit and serve it with a béarnaise sauce (see "Sauces and Marinades") and sautéed potatoes.

fillet with red wine

This is a fancy spitted tenderloin—the sort of thing you might cook for a very special occasion. Buy a whole fillet and some suet, pounded into a flat, thin sheet, a half pound of smoked tongue and some salt pork. Cut the salt pork and the tongue into matchstick-size pieces. With a larding needle prick large holes in the surface of the meat and force pieces of the pork and tongue into these holes. This is called "piquéing" and it adds a great deal to the flavor of a roast. Sprinkle the meat well with freshly ground black pepper and add a touch of rosemary or rosemary seasoning powder. Spit the roast and wrap the suet around it lightly for the first 25 minutes of cooking. (Or you can spread it well with fat instead.) Baste it every 10 or 15 minutes with pan drippings mixed with red wine.

Serve this fillet with a good green salad and some potatoes baked in coals, or sautéed potatoes. I like to add a dish of fresh mushrooms cooked in butter and flavored with a little garlic. For this meal a fine red wine is as necessary as cabbage is for corned beef.

SEASONINGS

■ If your roast is the best aged beef and an excellent cut, you need nothing but coarse-ground salt and fresh-ground pepper to bring out its fine flavor. However, if you want extra zip, try one of the following three suggestions:

1. Rub the meat, flesh and fat both, with dry mustard. Baste with fat from the dripping pan and dry mustard mixed together.

2. Rub the meat with a little dried or fresh rosemary, or sprinkle it with rosemary seasoning powder (I like the Spice Islands brand). Rosemary and beef have a special affinity.

3. Do a roast version of French pepper steak. Press freshly ground black pepper in large quantities into the roast firmly so that it will stick. Baste with the fat and the peppery outside will turn crusty and the flavor of the pepper will permeate the whole roast.

If you are afraid your piece of beef may lack flavor and be a little tough, make a coating of soy sauce, a healthy sprinkling of grated fresh ginger, grated garlic and a little rosemary seasoning powder. Roll the

roast around in this and fork some of it into the flesh. Let it stand for a while and when you roast it, baste with some of the fat from the drippings, a little soy sauce and red wine mixed. Do not salt the roast, as the soy sauce substitutes for salt.

Try any of the marinades suggested in the chapter on sauces and baste the roast with the marinade while it is cooking.

yorkshire pudding

Yorkshire pudding is something like a popover. It can be light, eggy and delicate or it can be as soggy and tough as a wet blanket. In the days before the patent oven, this dish was cooked right in the dripping pan under the roasting beef, and in many parts of England it is still done this way in the oven. The batter is simply poured into the hot beef drippings and the pudding cooks as the roast drips additional juices onto it. Of course it's very rich, but it's wonderful eating.

My recipe: Beat 2 eggs until they are fluffy, then beat in 1 cup of milk. Stir in 1 cup of sifted flour and mix until there are no lumps. Finally add 1 teaspoon of freshly ground black pepper, 1 teaspoon of salt and about 3 tablespoons of beef drippings. Pour the batter into a hot pan or ring mold which has been well oiled with drippings and bake in a hot (450°) oven for 20 minutes. Reduce the heat and continue baking at 325° for another 15 to 20 minutes. It should be browned and puffy.

Another way to cook Yorkshire pudding is in front of the fire, on barbecue grills that have the firebox in back of the spit. Pour a good deal of the juice from the dripping pan into a baking pan, pour the pudding batter into the baking pan and bake it in front of the fire. You will probably have to transfer it to the oven for the last few minutes to get it really brown and puffy.

43

LAMB

■ A leg of lamb should be cooked rare to medium; it should never be well done. Whoever started well-done lamb did the animal a great deal of harm. It is very hard to get baby lamb in this country unless you live in a community where there is a Greek or Italian butcher. Lamb is graded, as is beef, U.S. Prime, U.S. Choice, etc. For lamb, estimate approximately three-quarters of a pound of meat per person. You may have a leg boned and tied with the shankbone left in, or spitted with the bone in. The former is much easier for the inexperienced carver.

leg of lamb, french style

Make several gashes with a sharp knife in the leg of lamb and insert slivers of garlic. Rub the roast with salt, pepper and a little rosemary. Spit, balance and roast over a medium fire until the internal temperature reads 140° to 145° for rare lamb. This business of cooking it to 180° is destructive. Remove from the heat and let it rest or coast for 10 minutes or so before carving.

stuffed leg of lamb

Have the butcher bone the leg except for the shankbone. Take along several cloves of peeled garlic, 2 or 3 strips of bacon and a few sprigs of fresh mint. Before the roast is rolled and tied, ask the butcher to place these inside. Spit and roast.

rack of lamb

The rack makes a delicious roast, though it is a little more delicate in flavor than most other cuts. It must be boned so that the spit will go through it. Season it well with garlic, salt and pepper and roast it until it is done but still rare. Serve with plenty of peas and new potatoes cooked in their jackets and liberally buttered.

shoulder of lamb

Shoulder of lamb, boned and rolled, can be prepared in any of the ways suggested for leg of lamb. Here is another stuffing that you might like to use with the shoulder. Heat 4 tablespoons of butter and add 1 or 2 cloves of garlic and 2 medium onions chopped up. Saute these until they are just soft. Add 1½ cups of bread crumbs, ¼ pound of sausage meat which has been cooked for 5 minutes in a little hot water and then drained, and 1 teaspoon of fresh or dried tarragon. Blend well and spread the shoulder with this mixture. Roll it up, tie it securely, season and spit it. Roast according to the directions above. Serve with roasted or sautéed potatoes, and perhaps some corn on the cob.

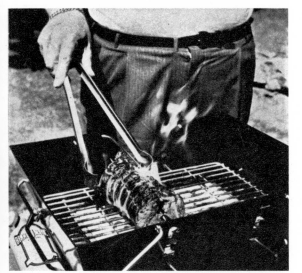

Sear shoulder of lamb on the propane grill's lower rack, foil-cook it on the upper

foiled shoulder of lamb

A boned and rolled shoulder may be broiled on a propane grill if it is seared on the lower rack, wrapped in foil and cooked on the upper rack for approximately 30 to 40 minutes. The shoulder should be turned several times during the cooking.

shoulder of lamb orientale

Combine ½ cup of Japanese soy sauce, ½ cup of sherry or Madeira, 3 cloves of garlic finely chopped, ¼ cup of finely grated fresh ginger. If fresh ginger is not available, use ¼ cup of preserved or candied ginger. Marinate a boned and rolled shoulder of lamb in this mixture, turning frequently for 24 hours. Spit, balance and roast, basting occasionally with the marinade until the internal temperature of the meat reaches 140° to 145°.

saddle of lamb

Saddle of lamb is an ideal cut for a party where you wish to impress. Insert slivers of garlic in the saddle which the butcher has tied and secured for you. (Have lamb kidneys stuffed into the saddle if you wish.) Spit the saddle parallel to the bone and roast over medium heat until the internal temperature reaches 140° to 145°. A saddle is sliced in thin slices parallel to the backbone. The fillet and the kidneys, if they are used, should be removed at the same time.

45

A properly balanced leg of lamb should look like this

baron of lamb

Baron of lamb includes the saddle and two legs. In other words, it is the hind quarter.

If you can find young lamb, it makes a spectacular and exciting roast for a large number of people. Tie the legs together securely and insert slivers of garlic in the flesh. Rub the joints well with salt, freshly ground pepper and rosemary. Balance on a spit and roast until the internal temperature reaches 140° to 145°. This is a heller to carve, for one has to cut parallel slices from the saddle and thin slices from the legs. So study your anatomy before you attempt a baron. Know where the bones come and where the fleshiest part of the roast is. Sautéed potatoes and tiny new potatoes are both excellent with lamb. Also the good traditional American baked beans (see page 95). Peas are a fine accompaniment and turnips are also excellent with this dish.

MUTTON

■ Mutton is not as well known in this country as it should be. If it is properly cooked it can be as delicious as any meat there is. For roasting on a spit, the leg and the saddle of mutton are probably the best cuts. The best mutton is usually very fat, and you will want to cut away much of the excess fat or it will clog your dripping pan during the cooking procedure.

Like lamb, mutton is improved by seasoning with garlic. Slash small holes in the flesh and insert bits of garlic clove. I like the herb called "Old Man" with mutton, but not many people have bushes of it in their gardens. Spit the roast and baste it with a combination of red wine and a little oil. The wine helps to cut some of the fat. Mutton should be well salted and sprinkled with freshly ground black pepper while roasting. Serve it rare. Like lamb, it is much better in flavor and texture when it is pink to red on the inside.

Perfect accompaniments to mutton are cole slaw and yellow turnips, boiled, mashed and heavily laced with butter—a remarkable combination of contrasting flavors.

mock venison

If this dish is properly prepared with a roast of mutton it can give you the excellent flavor of good venison without the toughness that venison sometimes has. Use game marinade (see the chapter on "Sauces and Marinades") and let the mutton soak in it for 2 days. When you are ready to cook it, remove it from the marinade, arrange it on the spit and roast it just to the rare stage. Use the marinade as a baste. Prepare a sauce by skimming all the fat from the drippings, adding any marinade that is left, 1 teaspoon of mustard, 1½ teaspoons of freshly ground black pepper and salt to taste. Bring all this to a boil and simmer gently for 5 minutes. Thicken with small balls of flour and butter kneaded together. Serve the mutton with the sauce, mashed turnips, potatoes and cole slaw.

saddle of mutton

I have found that you can easily spit a saddle of mutton without having it boned, provided it is heavily meated. You can piqué the meat with garlic or treat it like mock venison (see previous recipe). Season it, roast it rare, basting it frequently, and when it is done carve it the long way in thin strips. If you cut the saddle along the bone—parallel to the spinal bone—you will get the meat in thin, fine strips. Don't forget the delicious, tender fillet on the inside of the saddle.

PORK

■ Pork can be as delicious a meat as one can prepare on the outdoor grill if it is slow-roasted and well basted. The loin, the shoulder and the fresh ham all lend themselves to outdoor cooking. The fresh ham and shoulder should be boned, rolled and tied before balancing on the spit. If it is possible, the skin should be left on. Many Italian shops will stuff a boned and rolled fresh ham or shoulder with fresh basil, garlic, parsley and other savory bits, which makes for perfect spit roasting.

It is well to remember that pork must be cooked through. There must be an internal temperature of about 175° to 180° to ensure doneness without losing the desirable natural juices.

loin of pork

Buy a whole loin of pork and have it boned. Sprinkle the two halves with thyme, salt and pepper, and add some onion slices. Tie it together securely, spit it, and roast until the internal temperature reaches 175°. Meanwhile, baste the pork with drippings and a little beer. When done it should have a nice glaze on the outside. If you prepare some parsnips and sweet potatoes by boiling them in salted water until they are just short of done, and then add them to the dripping pan for the last half hour, you will find them a tasty addition to your roast pork. Mix freshly grated horse-radish and applesauce as a zippy accompaniment to cut the richness of the meat.

roast fresh ham

If you have the time and the patience, a whole fresh ham on the spit will give you a truly succulent feast. The fire must not be too hot, for the meat must cook slowly. Have your butcher leave the skin on the ham and bone it and tie it for you. Score the skin in diamond shapes or in strips so that it will form crisp bits of cracklings as the ham cooks. Salt and pepper the meat well and rub a little thyme or thyme seasoning powder into the surface. Sprinkle it with ground ginger, or fresh grated ginger if it is available.

Make a basting sauce of 1 cup of orange juice, ½ cup of lemon juice, 1 cup of oil or melted pork fat, 1 teaspoon of thyme, 1 tablespoon of grated fresh ginger or 1 teaspoon of ground ginger and 3 tablespoons of soy sauce. Arrange the ham on the spit and roast very slowly, basting often. The meat will take about 25 minutes or more per pound to cook. It should reach an internal temperature of 185° on a meat thermometer. Carve the ham in thin slices and put some of the crackling skin on each piece of meat.

With this serve thin slices of tart apple that have been sautéed in butter with a little sugar added, and sliced onions steamed in butter. Simply slice large onions in thick pieces, put them in a skillet with about 5 tablespoons of butter, cover and cook slowly until tender. Do not let them brown—just let them steam in their own juice and the melted butter. Just before serving, add ½ cup of grated cheese, preferably imported Swiss, to the onions.

spareribs

Soak spareribs in soy sauce for 1 hour. Rub these with chopped garlic or a little thyme or oregano. Arrange the whole sides of spareribs by lacing them on the spit in deep scallops. Figure on a pound of spareribs per person. They should be roasted over a slow fire for an hour to an hour and a half, and basted occasionally with the marinade. This makes them succulent and brings out the flavor.

chinese spareribs

If you have a Waring Blendor, combine 1 clove of garlic and a small can of Chinese bean sauce and a small can of Hoy Sin sauce, 1 teaspoon of salt and a drop of red coloring. Blend for 2 minutes and add to 1 cup of cooking oil and 1 cup of sugar. Marinate spareribs overnight or for several hours, turning them often in this mixture. Weave on spit and roast over medium fire, basting or brushing them with the marinade during the cooking process.

polynesian spareribs

Combine 4 teaspoons of dry mustard, ½ cup of sherry, ¼ cup of soy sauce and 2 cups of apricot jam. Add to this 1 teaspoon each of ground cloves, fennel, aniseseed and cinnamon. Coat the spareribs well with this mixture and let them stand for an hour. Weave them on the spit and roast over a slow fire, brushing them occasionally with the marinade. (Note: Potatoes cooked in the ashes, grilled tomatoes and sauerkraut go exceptionally well with spareribs.)

roast suckling pig

Suckling pigs range in size from around 9 to 18 or 20 pounds and it takes a rather large spit to roast one. If you have ample equipment, here is an excellent way to do it:

Choose a pig weighing about 12 pounds and clean it thoroughly. Sprinkle the inside with salt, freshly ground pepper and a little oregano or sweet basil. Rub the skin well with oil and salt and a little of the same herb. Arrange the pig on the spit so that it is perfectly balanced and roast for 2 to 2½ hours, basting often with the pan drippings. Some people like to prepare the skin with a mixture of honey, lemon juice and oregano.

Serve it with sauerkraut which you have steamed in beer and seasoned with garlic and coarse black pepper. Pass around a heaping dish of ice-cold applesauce. Beer is an excellent drink with this dish.

Here's how to carve the pig: Cut along the spinal column, cutting the pig in half. Remove each ham. Slice the hams and cut through the ribs. Serve each person a little of the rib meat and a little of the ham.

Traditionally, suckling pig is decorated before it is brought to the table. A necklace of raw cranberries, two cranberries for the eyes and an apple in the mouth is the usual thing. I'm just as happy with suckling pig served without a costume.

Small birds like squab or large ones like ducks are at their very best

POULTRY

when you broil, baste and serve them piping hot, right from the grill

The various birds classified as poultry take easily to the barbecue or grill. They should be split carefully and the backbone or spinal column should be removed completely, so that the *halves* roast easily on the grill. It is my belief that halved birds cook best if they are brushed liberally with butter, oil or a favorite sauce and placed on the grill bone-side-down. About halfway through the broiling process, turn the skin side to the heat and continue the broiling. If the birds are not moist or fat, it is a good idea to brush or baste them with butter, oil or sauce as they cook.

Small birds, such as squab or squab chicken, may be broiled whole with four or five turns during the broiling period. Larger birds, such as capon and turkey, may be halved or quartered for the broiling period and the same technique followed.

Parts of chickens or turkeys may be broiled. It is my feeling that they should be cooked in a basket type of grill. Serve broiled poultry right from the grill, when it is at its crisp, delicious best.

CHICKEN

broiled chicken

Have the butcher split your chickens for broiling and remove the backbone and the end part of the breastbone. This makes them lie much flatter on the grill. Rub the meat well with butter, salt, pepper and paprika. Grill bone-side-down. Turn once during the broiling to give the skin time to brown and crisp. Baste with melted butter. For a change, combine ½ lemon juice and melted butter. Chicken will take from 25 to 45 minutes, according to size. They are delicious served with sautéed or home-fried potatoes.

rosemary broiled chicken

Prepare chickens as above and broil bone-side-down. Before turning, dip the chickens into melted butter and press them into fresh rosemary leaves, turn and broil. When the broiling is finished, bring up the fire so that the leaves will char, imparting a fine scent of the herb.

51

oriental chicken

Marinate 4 chicken halves in 1 cup of soy sauce, 1 cup of sherry, 1 teaspoon of dry ginger or 2 tablespoons of grated fresh ginger, for 1 hour. Broil according to directions given above, basting with a little of the marinade from time to time. Just before the chickens are ready to serve, remove and press skin side into sesame seeds and return to the grill so that the seeds can toast.

TURKEY

roast turkey #1

Turkeys weighing 4 to 7 pounds will be excellent broiled. They must be split and cooked over low heat—far from the coals—for the first 40 minutes. Then they may be moved closer to the heat to finish cooking and browning.

Arrange the turkey halves bone-side-down on the grill and cook slowly for 25 minutes. Season to taste and turn skin-side-down. Continue cooking for 15 to 20 minutes, or until almost done. To finish cooking, bring meat close to the coals to brown. Baste during the cooking with a little seasoned oil.

The Borden Company

roast turkey #2

To serve 4 persons, buy a good-sized turkey broiler and have it split. Cook 1 pound of sliced bacon until it is crisp. Add salt, pepper and paprika to the bacon fat and keep it warm. Spread the bone side of the turkey halves with some of the bacon-fat mixture and grill according to instructions for Roast Turkey #1. Brush the skin side with bacon fat before turning. Brush the turkey twice more with bacon fat as you continue cooking it.

Serve the broiled turkey garnished with the bacon, tiny green peas cooked with onions and dressed with plenty of butter and potatoes boiled in their jackets. Follow this with cole slaw as a separate course. Dress the cabbage with a sauce of sour cream and fresh horse-radish. Fresh fruit and cheese, plus some strong hot coffee, make a perfect finish to this simple dinner.

grilled turkey parts

If you are fond of turkey but would rather not have it around for several days, purchase turkey parts and broil them according to rules for broiled turkey. Turkey thighs, if they are very large, may be spitted. They may also be boned, stuffed, rolled and tied as are the whole turkeys. For those who love dark meat—and there are millions of us—this is indeed a delicious treat.

DUCK

broiled duckling

With broiled duckling, many people miss the pleasure of eating crisply broiled halved ducklings, such as small-sized Long Island ducks. Have the butcher split them or split them yourself. Season with salt and pepper and broil bone-side-down for about 20 to 25 minutes. Turn for 10 minutes and return to bone side. The process will take from 45 to 55 minutes. Don't forget to increase the heat at the end of the broiling period to crisp the outside skin. Serve the duckling with rice, applesauce and a crisp green salad.

VARIATION: Duckling with olives. Combine ½ cup of finely chopped stuffed olives with ½ teaspoon of freshly ground black pepper and 2 tablespoons of softened butter. Force this mixture under the skin of halved ducklings and broil as above.

VARIATION: Curried duckling. Saute 2 tablespoons of finely chopped onion in 2 tablespoons of butter and oil, and add 1½ tablespoons of curry powder and ¼ cup of vermouth or sherry. Let this simmer for 5 minutes and add ½ cup of honey and the juice of 2 lemons. Broil duckling as above and brush with this mixture several times while it cooks.

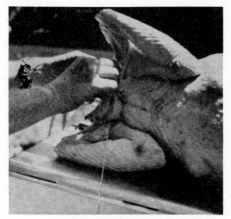

Turkey must be trussed and tied securely, then balanced on the spit

Baste the turkey frequently as you spit-roast it under the reflector hood

SPIT-ROASTED POULTRY

■ Spit-roasted chicken, turkey and duck have a flavor that no oven roasting can ever give them, plus a superb crispy skin. People have a tendency to overcook chickens, and this is true of spit roasting as well as oven roasting. A chicken is done when the leg and thigh joint move back and forth freely. This is really the only test you can make. With a large bird, the meat thermometer is inserted in the thick part of the thigh without touching the bone. It will register about 180° when the turkey or large chicken is ready.

The following general instructions may be followed for poultry and game on any spit-roasting unit; variations will be noted in the recipes for specific dishes:

1. Select young, plump, tender poultry and good-quality game.

2. Wash if necessary, remove hair and pinfeathers by singeing; dry well (inside and out) with soft cloth.

3. Season inside (not outside) according to taste; stuff if desired; close opening with poultry pins or skewers, or sew with strong thread.

4. Truss and tie securely. Tie string around legs, then cross over breast around wings and back to legs, or fasten wings to body and tie ends of legs together.

5. If you insert the skewer just in back of the tail of the bird and bring it out in the side of the breastbone, you will get a good balance for your bird. If you are doing two or more birds on the spit, alternate them with the breast of one against the leg of the next. One should be back on top, the next stomach on top, and so on.

CHICKEN

■ Young plump birds that are usually broiled make excellent eating if seasoned and roasted on a spit. If you buy the tiny broilers, figure one chicken to each serving. A good-sized broiler will serve two persons very nicely.

Butter the chickens well and rub them with a little tarragon seasoning powder—or use fresh tarragon if it is available. Sprinkle some of the herb inside the chickens, too. Truss the birds firmly so that they will hold their shape. Several of these tiny birds will fit on one spit. Be sure to arrange them on the spit so that they are properly balanced to ensure evenness of cooking.

Roast chickens from 30 minutes to 1 hour, depending on their size. I don't like chicken overdone—it loses some of its juiciness and flavor. For me, the meat at the joint of a perfectly done chicken still has a slightly pinkish cast.

I like to baste chicken with a mixture of melted butter and white wine, with salt and sometimes a little paprika added. This gives the birds a nice glaze and leaves delicious pan juices.

Serve these small chickens with plain watercress—no dressing on it— and crisp fried potatoes. To me, the usual gravy-and-mashed-potatoes is out of key with this delicate morsel.

VARIATION: Substitute rosemary for tarragon in the seasoning.

• Try stuffing the chicken with a few tiny white onions which have been peeled and browned in butter for about 10 minutes. Sew the chicken up before you truss it. Serve it with more tiny white onions cooked in butter until brown and just soft.

• Here is an excellent way to make an extra-fancy dish of broilers: Buy an extra half-pound of chicken livers for each four persons when you buy your broilers. Also buy a pound of veal and have it ground fine. Chop a small onion and sauté it in 4 tablespoons of butter. Add the veal and toss it around in the pan to separate it. Add the chicken livers chopped very fine (or you can have the butcher grind these too) and ½ cup of cognac or whisky and let the mixture simmer for 5 minutes. Add 1 cup of dry bread crumbs, a good dash of tarragon or tarragon seasoning powder, salt and 2 eggs. Mix well, stuff the chickens with the mixture and sew them up. Truss them, spit them and roast as above, basting with white wine and butter. These stuffed chickens will take a little longer to cook.

To serve, split each chicken in half, serve a half heaped with stuffing on each plate. Pour the pan juices over each serving. A good green salad is enough with this dish, which is rich and filling and doesn't need the addition of potatoes.

• The French have a very interesting method of preparing chicken under a roasting unit. For this dish use a chicken big enough to serve four people, or two of the larger broilers. Roast plain, basting with just a little melted butter and salt. When the chicken is cooked, remove it from the heating unit, pour over it 4 ounces of cognac and ignite to blaze. Put on a hot platter to carve.

Collect the drippings, add 1 cup of heavy cream and 3 egg yolks. Heat slowly over a low flame, stirring constantly. Be careful the sauce does not boil or it will curdle. When it is hot and nicely thickened, taste for seasoning and add a little cognac. Serve the sauce with the chicken and add rice and greens to make a delicious meal.

CAPON

■ A capon is a fat, tender bird—a choice dish for the table. It needs no embellishments and is best when served plain in all its delicious glory. A large capon weighs up to 8 or 9 pounds, and will not fit into many of the smaller grilling units. Following the trend in turkeys, capon raisers have been developing smaller birds which are just as fat and tender as the traditional big ones. Look for one that fits your cooking space. Simply truss it, spit it and roast it plain, basting with a little butter. Salt and pepper toward the end of the cooking process. Serve with crisp fried potatoes and watercress.

garlic chicken

Mash 2 cloves of garlic and blend with ¼ pound of butter. Let this stand for ½ hour. Meanwhile chop 2 more cloves of garlic very fine and sprinkle them inside the cavity of a chicken. Add a large sprig of parsley, a cube of butter and close the vent with foil. Truss the chicken well.

Melt the garlic butter, add the juice of 1 lemon and salt and pepper to taste. Roast the chicken on a spit, basting it frequently with the melted-butter mixture.

baby chickens on the spit

These little delicacies are called *poussin,* squab chicken or baby pullets. Plan at least one to a person, more for those with hearty appetites. Spit, brush with plenty of seasoned butter and roast them quickly, being careful not to overcook. Brush frequently during the cooking with melted butter.

If you are fortunate enough to have your own garden, dig a few hills of very small new potatoes. Cook them in their jackets and drench them with melted butter, salt and pepper. Add, if you wish, some chopped parsley or a few finely chopped chives. Tiny French peas are also an exquisite addition to this menu.

TURKEY

■ Small turkeys spitted and roasted are superb, but even a large 18-20-pound turkey can be cooked to perfection in this manner if you have the equipment to handle it. A turkey should be basted frequently, and my choice is melted butter with white wine or dry vermouth. Test doneness by moving the legs back and forth to see if they are loose. If you use a meat thermometer, remove the turkey at 170°-175°.

In buying turkey, plan at least 1 pound per person.

stuffed turkey

This will take a little longer to cook and must be perfectly balanced on your spit, so tie it securely.

The stuffing will take the place of a starch dish and cut down on the preparations for the dinner. Allow 1 cup of stuffing for each pound of turkey. For a 12-pound bird you will need 8 cups of rice (cooked). In 6 tablespoons of butter sauté 1 cup of finely chopped green onions and 1 cup of finely chopped parsley. Cook for about 5 minutes and add to the rice. Add also 1 cup of finely chopped chicken or turkey livers, 1 cup of finely chopped ham, 1 cup of chopped pistachio nuts, 1 teaspoon of rosemary, salt and pepper to taste, ½ cup of melted butter and 1 cup of Madeira or ½ cup of cognac.

Stuff the turkey lightly and sew up the vent or close it with small skewers. Remove the neck and secure the skin at the neck cavity in the same manner. Truss the bird, rub it with seasoned butter, spit it and roast it as you would chicken. Baste it during the roasting with melted butter mixed with white wine, dry vermouth, Madeira or cognac.

If you want to take the trouble to make a giblet gravy in the kitchen and bring it out, it is quite good served on the stuffing. Also, if you feel in the mood, a huge bowl of mashed potatoes would grace this meal.

roast turkey flambé

This dish has an exceptionally delicious sauce and makes fine party fare; guests are apt to ask you for the recipe.

Roast the turkey according to the above instructions, basting well with melted butter and white wine. When it is done, remove it to a hot flameproof platter or a board. Heat ¼ cup of cognac slightly, pour it over the turkey and ignite. When the flames die down, pour off the juices into a cup. Keep the turkey warm. Sauté the chopped giblets briefly in 4 tablespoons of butter. (Do this in a pan on the grill, in an electric skillet or in a chafing dish.) To the giblets add the reserved juices and a little of the giblet broth. Taste for seasoning, blend well and heat thoroughly. Stir in 1½ cups of sour cream, blend and heat, but do not allow this mixture to boil or it will curdle. Add another dash of cognac and serve with the turkey.

rolled roast turkey

This is a popular method for spitting or roasting turkeys nowadays. Have your butcher do it or try this process yourself. (Note: In some cities, rolled and tied turkeys are available in supermarkets and poultry shops, ready for the oven.) If you do it yourself, skin the turkey, trying to keep the skin intact, then bone the turkey, keeping it as whole as

possible. If you start from the side of the backbone and work with sharp knives along the bones, you will not find this a difficult job. Lay the boned turkey meat on the skin. Season with salt, pepper, tarragon and spread well with softened butter. Roll tightly and tie firmly with butcher's twine. Rub with butter or oil and spit and balance it. Cook until the meat thermometer registers about 175°, then let it rest for about 15 minutes before removing from the spit. Turkey prepared this way is perfect for carving.

DUCK

domestic duck

To prepare Long Island duckling and other domestic varieties, spit the duckling and roast until nearly done. Baste during the last few minutes with a mixture of 2 tablespoons of soy sauce, 4 tablespoons of sherry, white wine or whisky, 2 tablespoons of honey and a few slivers of ginger. This will give the crisp skin a nice flavor and a high glaze. The duck will take about 1½ hours to cook.

To serve, cut in quarters with poultry shears or a heavy knife.

VARIATION: You may vary the basting sauce by adding curry powder to taste, garlic to taste, a little orange juice and grated orange rind, or use any of the sauces given under the recipes for broiled duckling.

GOOSE

■ Goose, unfortunately an almost forgotten delicacy, is a national delight. Roasting on a spit is an excellent method for cooking geese, since it retains the moisture but eliminates much of the fat.

Select a good fat goose. Cut away the excess fat from the inside. Render it and save. Rub the interior with half a lemon, and then with thyme seasoning powder and salt. Add a couple of onions and sew up the goose. Balance it, arrange it on the spit and be sure it is well placed. Roast it without basting. Prick the skin in several places to let the fat escape. Watch the dripping pan. The fat will collect there at a great rate and it must be emptied. Test the goose for doneness by puncturing the thigh with a sharp fork. When the juice no longer runs pinkish the bird is done. It should take about 2 hours to cook, and when done the skin should be very crisp and brown.

Serve goose with puréed chestnuts heated with butter, and sauerkraut cooked for several hours with white wine. The tang of the kraut is just what is needed to cut the richness of goose.

VARIATION: Try stuffing your goose with as much garlic as it will hold. Sew up the vent and roast as above. Remove garlic before eating.

Whether bought or caught, seafood takes to barbecuing. Broil it; spit

FISH AND
SHELLFISH

Fishermen and ardent campers are never at a loss to cook their catch. Those to whom outdoor cooking is a new experience will be delighted with what they can do with fish on an outdoor grill. One thing to remember always—fish should not be overcooked. Because of their delicate meat, small fish should be grilled in a hinged grill which makes them easier to handle. Good-sized spatulas or pancake turners are a big help in turning large fish on a grill. Plenty of lemon is a necessity with fish. Good butter and olive oil also make for better results.

GRILLING WHOLE FISH

■ This method can be used for practically any type of fish. Small fish need a brisker heat than large fish, because of the shorter cooking time. I like to butter or oil the inside of a fish and season it with salt and pepper. A few slices of onion or a sprig of dill or tarragon inside the fish before broiling gives it a delicious taste. Thin, thin slices of lemon or even orange are excellent.

Oil your grill or your hinged grill well before you start to cook. I find that if you brown the fish well on both sides and continue cooking, turning often, it will be evenly cooked. If you feel that the fish is too dry, baste with a mixture of olive oil and lemon juice.

Fish is cooked when the flesh flakes easily when you test it with a fork, a skewer or a toothpick. Small fish will cook in 10 to 15 minutes. Larger fish will take up to 60 minutes to cook. Lemons, parsley butter, anchovy butter, hollandaise or béarnaise sauce are excellent complements to grilled fish. Plain boiled or crisp French fried potatoes are traditional accompaniments.

fish flambé

In the Mediterranean countries, fish are grilled and removed to a hot platter or a bed of rock salt covered with herbs. They are then topped with dried herbs, usually fennel, dill, rosemary, thyme or parsley. Sprigs of these dried herbs are used. Two to three ounces of cognac are poured over them and ignited. The burning of the alcohol will light the dried

61

Trout, brushed with parsley butter before grilling, are a gourmet's delight

herbs, which will tease the taste buds through the nostrils and impart a subtle, delicious flavor to the fish. This process may be used with any small or large fish.

filleted fish flambéed
A new and sensational restaurant in New York, The Forum of the Twelve Caesars, uses a small Chinese *wok* (a rounded vessel used over charcoal for which you can buy a rack) and herbs aglow to finish off broiled fillets of perch. The fish is then flambéed and served with a sauce of chopped shallots, butter and white wine.

spitted fish
Large fish such as salmon, haddock, cod, tuna, sturgeon and some members of the bass family may be spitted and roasted over charcoal. The fish must be tied securely or wired to the spit. Some people make a wire basket, which they line with ferns, that will fit on the spit. Baste the fish with olive oil and lemon juice blended together.

foil-roasted fish
Whole fish may be rolled in aluminum foil which has been buttered or oiled and either roasted directly in the coals or roasted on the grill.

The advantage of using foil is that you may stuff the fish with any savory stuffing you desire, or with thinly sliced raw onions, peppers, tomatoes and sprigs of parsley, well lubricated with butter or oil, and know that the juices will not run out and that you will have a perfectly flavored fish when it is finished. Note: Small fish may be cooked in the same manner, although I recommend a double coating of foil for them.

fish steaks and filleted fish

Fish steaks, especially those from the oilier fish, make delicious charcoal-broiled main courses. I like a steak cut from 1½ to 2 inches thick; and for my favorite fish, I must put salmon first, sturgeon second, swordfish third, halibut fourth. The steak as well as the grill on which it is cooked should be oiled, and the coals should be moderate. Total cooking time, allowing for turning the fish over once during the process, should be from 12 to 15 minutes, depending upon the thickness and the texture of the steak. You may brush the fish while it is cooking with hot olive oil or melted butter. Salt, freshly ground pepper and lemon butter may also be used. Fish may be rolled in crumbs, in chopped almonds or in sesame seeds during the broiling and returned to the grill.

marinated fish

Marinate fish steaks in olive oil which has been cut with lemon juice and flavored with tarragon, dill, tomato purée or finely chopped garlic.

foil-cooked steaks

Fish steaks may be cooked in foil on top of the grill or in the coals. They are delicious combined with butter and thinly sliced tomatoes and cooked 7 to 10 minutes near the coals; turn them several times.

SHELLFISH

broiled whole lobster

Lobster is usually split before broiling, but it is my belief that this results in dry lobster meat, tasteless and tough. Broil the lobster whole over coals, allowing about 15 to 20 minutes cooking time. Turn it to cook evenly. Split it after broiling, remove the intestines and stomach and serve with plenty of melted butter and lemon quarters.

broiled split lobster

You may split live lobsters and spread them lavishly with softened butter and sprinkle with salt, pepper and paprika. Turn them flesh side down for about 3 minutes, then turn, spread on more softened butter and continue grilling. The whole process should take from 15 to 20 minutes, depending on the size of the lobsters. I like fried bread crumbs, melted butter and lemon juice, and crisp French fried potatoes with my broiled lobster.

soy-soaked shrimp

Choose the very largest shrimps you can find. Split them through the back with sharp scissors and marinate them in equal quantities of soy sauce and vermouth for 2 hours. Remove from the marinade and broil for 3 to 4 minutes on the grill. Have a collection of sauces, a garlic and anchovy butter, a highly seasoned mayonnaise and a rich sherry-flavored tomato sauce. Peel the shrimp with your fingers, drop into your favorite sauce and eat.

broiled shrimp appetizer

Allow 3 to 4 of the large shrimp per person. If only the smaller are available, you will need about 6 per person.

With sharp scissors cut down the back of each shrimp shell and remove the vein. Wash the shrimp thoroughly and place them in a large bowl. Over them pour 1 cup of olive oil, the juice of 3 lemons, ¼ cup of soy sauce, ¼ cup of finely chopped parsley and 3 tablespoons of fresh or dried tarragon. Let the shrimp stand in this mixture for 2 hours, tossing them around now and then so that they will be evenly marinated.

When you are ready to cook them, arrange them in basket grills and cook over hot coals for 5 or 6 minutes, turning twice. They should be tender and moist with slightly charred shells.

Frozen king crab legs—a spectacular yet simple dish—should be brushed with a

dill-flavored shrimp

Soak large split shrimp in white wine or dry vermouth to which you have added finely chopped garlic and fresh dill. After 2 hours remove them from the marinade and broil 3 to 4 minutes. Serve the shrimp with dill-flavored mayonnaise and thinly sliced cucumbers marinated in olive oil, vinegar, salt and pepper.

charcoal baked oysters

Arrange unopened oysters on the grill above a moderate charcoal fire. It will take anywhere from 6 to 8 minutes for the shells to open. Oysters must not overcook but they must heat through. Any type of restaurant oyster, especially the larger ones from the New Jersey or Delaware coast or the extremely large Pacific oysters, is suitable for this particular treat. Each oyster may be served with melted butter, anchovy butter, tarragon butter, or with horse-radish-flavored hollandaise. Thin rye-bread slices, well buttered, are a perfect accompaniment.

broiled king crab legs

King crab legs may be purchased frozen in many parts of the country. The large legs should be slit in the soft part of the shell. They should be grilled with the split side up. I like to brush them lavishly with a mixture of melted butter, lemon or lime juice and tarragon and merely heat them through, for they are already cooked before they are frozen. They really need, as do most grilled shellfish, French fried potatoes and crisp cucumbers for an accompaniment.

mixture of butter, lemon juice and tarragon and heated through on the grill

VARIETY
MEATS

Accent

are seeking exciting new barbecue dishes to offer guests and family

Liver, whole or sliced, kidneys and heart all lend themselves to charcoal grilling and are particularly delicious eating. If you're a hunter and bag a deer or two, you may apply the rules for calf's liver to deer liver and find it a rare treat. Since all variety meats are perishable, it is better to grill them in the garden rather than to transport them long distances. They usually are enhanced by a sharp sauce.

LIVER

broiled liver steaks

■ Calf's liver, good lamb liver and, at times, baby beef liver are all excellent for liver steaks. These should be cut 1 to 3 inches thick and should be fresh, not frozen, liver.

Butter the slices and broil quickly over a moderate fire, charring well on the outside and cooking the inside to your preferred state of rareness. I believe that liver is much more delicious when well charred and quite pink in the center. Serve liver steak with a béarnaise sauce or with garlic butter. A huge bowl of thickly sliced tomatoes and sliced raw onions makes a fine accompaniment.

stuffed liver rolls

Have the butcher cut thin slices of liver and cover each one with a thin slice of ham—preferably Italian prosciutto. Roll the liver slices around the prosciutto and secure with small skewers or toothpicks. Brush well with melted butter and grill over moderate coals, turning several times during the grilling. The liver should be pinky rare and the ham just heated through.

spitted liver

Use a whole calf's liver or lamb's liver. Roll the liver with rashers of bacon around it and tie it securely. Balance it on the spit and roast it over moderate coals until the internal temperature registers about 150°. Slice this delicious liver very thin. Serve with béarnaise sauce or chive butter, French fried potatoes and a crisp salad.

KIDNEYS

■ The only kidneys that to me are palatable for outdoor grilling are veal kidneys and lamb kidneys. You will find lamb kidneys in the skewer-cookery section.

broiled veal kidneys

You may leave some of the fat on veal kidneys if you wish—in fact, for charcoal grilling, I find it is wiser to do so. Either split the kidneys or cut them in 3 slices, depending on the size. Remove the core, and if you prefer a mild-flavored kidney, soak them in milk for an hour. (Veal kidneys, in my opinion, do not need this.) Brush the kidneys with melted butter or olive oil and grill them very quickly, since overcooked kidneys are always tough. Kidneys should be pleasantly browned on the outside. Salt and pepper them before serving. I like them with olive butter and sautéed potatoes.

deviled kidneys

Slice kidneys 1 to a person in 3 slices, keeping some of the fat on them. Broil as above and just before they are done, roll in fried bread crumbs and return to the grill to brown very quickly. Serve with a devil sauce.

Other kidneys will be found in the skewer-cookery section.

HEART

broiled heart

Clean and split a lamb heart or veal heart. Marinate with 1 teaspoon of salt, 1 teaspoon of freshly ground black pepper, 1 medium-sized onion thinly sliced, 2 cloves of garlic finely chopped and 1 teaspoon of rosemary leaves. Marinate for one hour and brush well with olive oil. Grill quickly so that you get a pleasantly charred surface on the outside and a nice pinkness on the inside. Serve with garlic butter and rice pilaf.

helen brown's heart hamburger

Clean a beef heart and put it through a food chopper. Season with salt and pepper, form into patties. Brush with butter and wrap in aluminum foil. Broil on the grill as you would hamburgers. Serve in the foil, accompanied by potatoes cooked in the ashes and quantities of butter.

ITALIAN SAUSAGES

■ Sweet and hot Italian sausages are delicious grilled over charcoal. Poach them for 5-8 minutes before grilling to cook out excess fat. They then grill quickly and to a delicious brownness. Have both sweet and hot sausages. Serve with crisp Italian bread and, if you wish, a great bowl of green noodles with butter and grated cheese.

SHORTRIBS

broiled shortribs
I find that broiled Prime or Choice grade shortribs are a very pleasant change from other meats. They are sturdy and not always as tender as other meats, but they have a delicious flavor. If I am buying a large roast of beef, I usually have it cut short and use the ends of the ribs for broiling. Or sometimes it is possible to get an excellent piece of shortrib from the butcher.

broiled shortribs in red wine marinade
Brush 5 pounds of shortribs with prepared mustard. Sprinkle with 2 cloves of garlic finely chopped, 1 teaspoon of dried basil or ¼ cup of fresh basil finely chopped. Add ½ cup of chopped parsley. Cover with red wine. Add 2 or 3 bay leaves and marinate for 24 hours. Remove from marinade, dry on paper towels, broil slowly until the ribs are well browned and crisp on the outside. Serve with fresh horse-radish grated into sour cream and tiny new potatoes steamed in butter.

American Molasses Company

One of the tastiest ways to broil vegetables, meats and seafood is on

SKEWER
COOKERY

Dudley-Anderson-Yutzy

Broiling on skewers is one of the oldest known forms of cookery. The early nomadic peoples of Asia and the Near East strung pieces of meat and vegetables on sticks and cooked them over the fire. This was the forerunner of the popular skewer cookery of today. For centuries the Japanese have cooked on skewers over the *hibachi*—a cast-iron tub with a grill over its top, set in a small decorative table or on a stand that can be used on a table. The charcoal is ignited outdoors in the *hibachi*, which is brought indoors after the charcoal has stopped smoking and turned to glowing coals.

The Skotch Grill is similar in operation to the *hibachi*. It too can be used in or out of doors and can be carried in the car to any picnic spot. It can be used for cooking on skewers as well as for grilling steaks, chops, fish, hamburgers and broiler-size poultry.

The French have cooked on skewers for generations. They call it *en brochette,* and many of the choice items on the menus in French restaurants are cooked this way. This type of cookery can be done in front of or above your charcoal fire, or in any broiler or electric grill. Some of the new grills have wheels with several skewers attached for cooking dishes *en brochette.* If you buy your own skewers you have a wide choice, from the simplest functional types to fancy designs copied from decorative old French *brochettes.*

Many foods cooked on skewers should be marinated for from several hours up to a day or so before grilling. Others, such as the *hibachi* recipes, are marinated for only ½ hour to 2 hours.

The ceramic grill heated with propane gas is also an excellent medium for skewer cookery. Follow the directions in the handbook which accompanies the ceramic grill.

VEGETABLES

■ Fresh vegetables may be combined and strung on skewers, brushed with oil or butter and broiled over charcoal. Almost any combination you like may be cooked this way. For example, eggplant sections, tomato wedges and mushrooms. The same combination may be used with onion

71

Almost any combination of vegetables strung on skewers will make a delicious

sections. Onions, tomatoes, partly cooked or canned potatoes, green-pepper slices, tiny whole parboiled onions are all excellent for skewer cookery—in fact, the combinations of vegetables that can be used are practically endless.

BEEF

tenderloin

Buy tenderloin or fillet in one piece. Cut in cubes 1½ x 2 inches. Arrange these on skewers, alternating with mushroom caps and chunks of onion, if you wish. Season with salt and pepper and brush with melted beef fat. (Get some suet at the butcher's and melt it, if you don't have any in your refrigerator.) Grill quickly over charcoal or in your electric unit until the meat is nicely browned but rare and juicy inside. This should take from 4 to 6 minutes. Serve with potatoes fried in beef fat, a large bowl of greens and French bread.

sirloin, moyen age

Cut your sirloin steak into cubes 1½ x 2 inches. Dust well with rosemary seasoning powder or roll in dried rosemary. Season with salt and alternate the chunks on skewers with small ripe tomatoes or tomato wedges. Grill quickly over charcoal or in the electric unit. Turn several times to cook evenly. Serve with a salad of cold string beans and finely chopped onion and a good French dressing. Fried potatoes or baked stuffed potatoes go well with this dish.

dish. Alternate them on the skewer, brush with oil or butter, and grill

tenderized beef

Buy a chunk of one of the tougher cuts of beef—chuck or round.
Cut it into cubes and sprinkle each cube with Adolph's Meat Tenderizer
(I prefer the non-seasoned). Use 1 teaspoon per pound and let the meat
stand at room temperature for 1 hour. Arrange on skewers, alternating
with mushroom caps or chunks of onion. Brush with melted beef fat
and season with salt and pepper. Broil over charcoal or in your electric
unit until nicely browned on all sides but still rare in the middle. Serve
with crisp French fried onions and French bread.

marinated beef

1. Marinate cubes of beef in olive oil and chopped onion. Roll them
in coarsely ground or cracked black pepper. Alternate the cubes on
skewers with small tomatoes or mushrooms. Broil until nicely browned
on all sides but rare in the center.

2. Marinate thin strips of beef fillet in soy sauce seasoned with grated
garlic. Sprinkle with black pepper, loop onto skewers and broil quickly.

3. Cut thin strips of sirloin or tenderloin, about 4 inches long and 1
inch wide. Roll each strip around—alternately—a stuffed olive, an oyster
(lightly puffed in hot water), a small parboiled onion or a mushroom
cap. Fasten each with a toothpick, brush with melted butter, and arrange
3 or 4 on a skewer. Broil quickly and season with salt and pepper.

4. Make a paste with horse-radish, grated onion, a little dry mustard
and red wine. Marinate cubes of tender beef in this for about 2 hours.
Arrange on skewers, season with salt and pepper and broil until browned

73

on the outside but still rare in the center. Brush with the paste once during the broiling.

5. Skewer cubes of beefsteak with tiny onions, tiny tomatoes and small canned potatoes. Add small hunks of beef fat here and there on the skewer. Brush with melted butter, and broil quickly. Season to taste.

SEAFOOD

fish

Fish fillets can be laced onto skewers, looped back and forth, and broiled in the following ways:

1. Brush with melted butter, season with salt and pepper and broil until just a pale golden brown. Add a dash of lemon juice.

2. Dip the fillets in melted butter and roll them in bread crumbs before looping them on skewers. Broil, and just before they are done season them with salt and pepper and dust them heavily with grated cheese—Swiss or Parmesan.

3. Marinate the fillets in olive or vegetable oil and lemon juice. Arrange them on skewers, sprinkle with salt, pepper and grated onion.

4. Marinate the fillets in oil and lemon juice. Roll them in grated onion and ginger, season with salt and tarragon seasoning powder. Skewer and broil.

5. Roll strips of bacon around the fillets, arrange them on skewers and broil.

6. Place a piece of boiled ham and a thin slice of dill pickle on each fillet and roll it up tightly. Fasten with a toothpick. Skewer, dip in melted butter and broil.

oysters

Oysters should first be just barely puffed in boiling water. Then follow any of these six methods:

1. String oysters on skewers, season with salt and pepper, dip into melted butter or bacon fat and broil.

2. Season the oysters, dip them in melted fat and roll in dry bread or cracker crumbs. String on skewers and broil.

3. Season the oysters, dip in melted fat and roll them in crumbs to which you have added grated Parmesan cheese, chopped parsley and a little garlic. String on skewers and broil.

4. Season the oysters, dip them in melted butter seasoned with curry powder, chopped onion and garlic. Then roll them in crumbs mixed with a little additional curry powder. String on skewers and broil.

5. Roll each oyster in a small piece of bacon; skewer and broil.

6. Dip the oysters in melted butter, roll them in grated Parmesan cheese and alternate the oysters on skewers with pieces of ham. Broil.

shrimp

1. Marinate giant shrimp in a barbecue sauce (see "Sauces and Marinades"). Skewer them, shell and all, and broil, basting with the sauce. They will take about 5 minutes to cook. Serve with the sauce and pass around plenty of large paper napkins.

2. Shell raw shrimp, wrap each one in a piece of bacon, and alternate them on skewers with black olives. Broil.

3. Alternate shelled shrimp on skewers with small tomatoes or tomato wedges. Dip in melted fat, season with salt and pepper and dust with chopped parsley and grated garlic. Broil, basting with more melted fat.

4. Marinate shelled raw shrimp in melted butter and oil seasoned with curry powder and chopped garlic. Roll in curry powder, season with salt and pepper, run them on skewers and broil.

5. Alternate shelled raw shrimp on skewers with oysters and scallops. Season and brush with melted butter. Broil.

6. Use shelled raw shrimp and scallops alternated on skewers, season, dip in melted butter and then roll in crumbs. Broil and serve with a hot sauce (see "Sauces and Marinades").

Take giant shrimp, marinated in barbecue sauce, and skewer them, shell and all

Broil them, using the extra barbecue sauce as a baste; serve on the skewers

barbecued shrimp no. 1

Select large shrimp—those that run 10 to 15 per pound—and peel them. String them on small skewers and marinate in a barbecue sauce for 1 hour. Broil over charcoal or in the electric grill for 3 to 5 minutes, turning once or twice during the cooking. (Of course, if you use regular rotisserie skewers, they will revolve by themselves.) Make a sauce to dunk them in of soy sauce, finely chopped onion and ginger and a little grated horse-radish.

barbecued shrimp no. 2

Peel and marinate the shrimp as above. Toast 4 ounces of sesame seeds and when the shrimp are removed from the marinade, roll them in the seeds before broiling on skewers. The flavor is delectable.

barbecued lobster

Cut the meat from 2 cooked lobster tails in thin chunks. Arrange these on small skewers. Marinate for 2 hours and cook very quickly over charcoal or under the electric grill.

barbecued oysters and clams

Arrange rows of oysters and clams on skewers and soak in barbecue sauce for 2 hours. Broil quickly over charcoal or in the electric grill. Serve with a highly seasoned sauce made with 1 cup of sour cream, 1 cup of mayonnaise, 2 crushed cloves of garlic, ¼ cup of chopped parsley, 1 teaspoon of salt, 1 tablespoon of Worcestershire sauce, 1 tablespoon of chopped tarragon, 1 teaspoon each of dry mustard and paprika.

scallops

1. Dip scallops in melted butter, season with salt and pepper and a dash of lemon juice. Broil on skewers until just lightly browned.
2. Wrap scallops in pieces of bacon, skewer and broil.
3. Dip scallops in melted butter, season and roll in curry powder. Add a dash of lemon juice and broil on skewers.
4. Marinate scallops in olive oil seasoned with soy sauce, lemon juice and grated garlic. Broil on skewers, brushing with the marinade.

SHISH KEBAB and SHASHLIK

shish kebab

Buy a leg or a shoulder of lamb. Although the leg is more expensive, it will give you more meat for your money. Figure about ½ to ¾ of a pound of meat per serving. This is lip-smacking food and people like generous amounts of it.

Cut the lamb into 2-inch-square cubes and marinate (see the chapter on "Sauces and Marinades") for a few hours or up to 48 hours. The longer they stand, the tastier they are. When you are ready to broil, arrange the cubes on skewers. You may use just meat or meat alternated with any of the following: onion chunks, tomato wedges or small whole tomatoes, mushroom caps, pineapple cubes or wedges, eggplant cubes, slices of zucchini, whole pickled onions.

Broil over charcoal or in the electric grill, turning often until nicely browned and crispy on the outside but still pink and juicy in the middle.

Serve with rice or *kasha* (steamed buckwheat, sold in grocery stores as groats), buttered toasted finger rolls, or French, Italian or Armenian bread heated slightly.

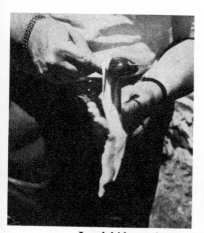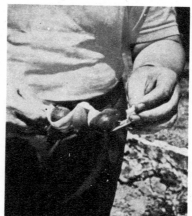

Lamb kidneys, bacon strips and mushroom caps make a mouth-watering trio

kidneys

Plan on 3 lamb kidneys to a person when you order from the butcher. Soak the kidneys in milk or salt water for 1 hour, then remove the core of gristle from each. Put 3 kidneys, covered with bacon strips, on each skewer. Add mushroom caps at each end of the skewer, and grill. Brush with melted butter, oil or English mustard during the grilling. Season with salt and pepper just before serving.

liver

Wrap small pieces of chicken, calf or lamb liver in pieces of bacon, run them on skewers and broil until the bacon is crisp.

shashlik

This recipe for the Russian form of shish kebab is from my favorite Russian restaurant in Paris, and it seems to me a delicious version.

Cut lamb in cubes, as above, and marinate up to 36 hours in olive oil to cover, seasoned with 4 finely chopped onions, 1 teaspoon of salt and 1 or more teaspoons of thyme. Arrange the shashlik on skewers and grill over charcoal or in the electric grill until nicely crisp on the outside but still pink and juicy in the middle. Serve with rice, small tomatoes and green onions.

JAPANESE DISHES

■ Many Japanese recipes lend themselves readily to outdoor and indoor barbecue cooking units. They are a delightful change and fun to do for guests. Always serve them with a big bowl of rice. If you can buy the wooden rice bowls from Japan, they are attractive, relatively unbreakable and will keep the rice hot for a long time.

To be truly authentic, most Japanese dishes call for long rice, which is really a gelatinous type of noodle that is cooked right in the meat dishes. It does not take the place of the bowl of rice and bears no resemblance to it. You may have to shop around to find this as well as the bean curd used in many Oriental dishes (see "Sources of Supply").

barbecued beef teriyaki

This can be a main course or you can use it for a hot snack with drinks. Buy 1½ pounds of tender beefsteak—sirloin or fillet—and cut it into thin strips. Prepare a sauce with ½ cup of soy sauce, 2 tablespoons of sherry, 3 tablespoons of sugar, 2 teaspoons of grated fresh ginger and 1 grated clove of garlic. Marinate the beef in this for 2 hours. String the meat on skewers or bamboo sticks and grill it over charcoal or under a broiler just long enough to sear on all sides. Baste with the sauce during the cooking.

VARIATION: Use small bite-size pieces of tender young chicken. Marinate for 1 or 2 hours and broil in a hinged grill until nicely browned and cooked through. Baste with the sauce.

VARIATION: Parboil spareribs for 25 minutes and then marinate in the sauce for an hour or so. Broil over charcoal until nicely browned, crisp and cooked through. Baste with the sauce. Parboiling the spareribs first saves cooking time at the grill and cuts down on the fat.

matsu kage yaki

This is the Japanese version of broiled chicken. Cut the meat from a 2½-pound broiler and slice it into thin strips. Marinate them in the following sauce for 2 hours: ½ cup of soy sauce, ½ cup of sherry, 3 tablespoons of sugar, 2 tablespoons of grated fresh ginger, ½ teaspoon of Mei Yen seasoning powder. When you are ready to broil the chicken, roll each piece in sesame seeds and broil on skewers over charcoal until nicely browned and cooked through.

beef hibachi

These are very popular cocktail snacks in Hawaii and on the Pacific coast, where they are cooked and served on tiny bamboo skewers. Small wooden or steel ones will do as well. For *hibachi* marinades, see "Sauces and Marinades."

Use good tender beef—sirloin or the best grade of rump steak—and cut the meat into 1½-inch strips. Then cut each strip into paper-thin slices, marinate in Hibachi Marinade No. 1 for about 2 hours, and string these on skewers. Broil over charcoal for seconds only. The heat should just curl the edges of the meat, crisp it a bit and give it a glaze. If you have more than one charcoal cooker—a couple of *hibachis* or Skotch Grills—you can let your guests do their own grilling. Simply pass a platter of the marinated meat on skewers and let them cook their own to taste.

Serve plenty of thin slices of buttered bread—rye, French, pumpernickel or Armenian bread—and slip the bits of meat off the skewers onto it. Pass bowls of hot mustard and Chinese sweet-and-sour sauce for condiments (see "Sauces and Marinades").

THE FULL MEAL

Appetites get sharp in the open air while guests wait for the meal to

APPETIZERS
AND SNACKS

ASTA

cook. An assortment of tasty snacks will stave off pangs of hunger

Half the fun of outdoor cooking is having an audience to admire your artistry. This means that guests must wait a while for their dinner. To keep them happily occupied, serve good, hearty drinks, along with plenty of substantial appetizers. Forget the quaint little canapés that the women's magazines feature. Instead, serve something easy to fix but satisfying. Here are some suggestions for dunks:

DUNK BOWLS

■ Serve any raw vegetables you like: cucumber strips, celery sticks, pepper strips, carrot sticks, cauliflowerets, asparagus tips, sliced turnips, green onions, radishes, endive or any other favorite. Put them in a bowl with ice to keep them crisp and let each guest help himself.

1. To 1½ cups of mayonnaise add 1 grated garlic clove, 1 chopped hard-boiled egg, the juice of a lemon, a dash of tarragon seasoning powder and 6 finely chopped scallions. Taste for seasoning and dilute with heavy cream to the right consistency.

2. Combine one 8-ounce jar of red caviar (the inexpensive kind) with 1 finely chopped large onion, ½ cup of soft bread crumbs which have soaked in ¼ cup of milk. Put this all into a blender or beat it with a heavy potato masher. It must be a thorough job of mixing. Add 1 cup of sour cream and mix again. This is a very highly seasoned dunk.

3. Combine 2 chopped cloves of garlic with ¼ cup of tiny white pickled onions (the kind used for cocktails) and 1 tin of anchovies coarsely chopped. Add 4 ounces of cream cheese and enough heavy cream or sour cream to thin it down.

4. To 1 pint of sour cream add ¼ cup of fresh dill finely chopped, salt to taste, ¼ cup of onion finely chopped and ½ cup of chopped parsley. Add a dash of lemon juice and let it stand for one hour. This also makes an excellent dressing for a salad of thin cucumber slices.

5. Take ½ cup of mayonnaise and ½ cup of sour cream, add ¼ cup of French's Mustard, 2 finely chopped garlic cloves, 1 teaspoon of tarragon, 2 tablespoons of finely chopped parsley and 2 tablespoons of finely chopped anchovies. Then add freshly ground black pepper to taste.

83

SEAFOOD SNACKS

■ There is nothing better than smoked or cured fish. I like the fresh-water fish—whitefish, carp, buffalo fish or chub—smoked or kippered. Serve it with lemon wedges and thin slices of salty rye or pumpernickel well buttered. Salmon, sturgeon and eel, also widely available, make perfect appetizers, too. So does herring, in all forms—marinated, in wine sauce, in sour cream, or smoked. Other delicious snacks are:

Sardines, French or Portuguese in olive oil, skinless and boneless in olive oil, spiced sardines, Norwegian sardines in olive oil, Maine sardines in soy-bean oil, California sardines in tomato or mustard sauce.

Fine tuna in olive oil is a wonderful snack on crackers or bread with lemon juice. Or it may be mixed with onion, chopped olives and mayonnaise for a spread.

Mussels, spiced and smoked, and smoked oysters from the Pacific coast make wonderful snacks or appetizers.

SAUSAGE AND PATE

■ Serve a big platter of several varieties of good sausage, thinly sliced, with thinly sliced buttered pumpernickel or rye bread—and dill pickles.

Here are suggestions for the sausage platter: salami, summer sausage, thuringer, metwurst, bologna, braunschweiger, cervelat, blood sausage, tongue sausage, mortadella, Lebanon bologna.

Serve a variety of mustards, too. You can make the hot English type by moistening dry mustard with a little white wine; you might also try some French Dijon mustard and some German or Dutch mustards.

Another good sausage appetizer is made by slicing cervelat very thin, combining it with greens and finely cut celery and dressing it with French dressing or mayonnaise. Add slices of tomato if you like.

patés

Buy a pound of the best liverwurst, mash it thoroughly with ¼ cup of finely chopped onion, 1 teaspoon of mustard, ¼ cup of heavy cream or sour cream and ¼ cup of whisky or cognac. The result tastes like a paté which would cost about four times as much. Put it in the electric beater or beat it with a fork and store it in the refrigerator.

country paté

Grind 1½ pounds each of pork liver and fresh pork. Combine with 1 large grated onion and 1 finely chopped clove of garlic. Add to this ½ cup of chopped parsley, 1 teaspoon of salt, 1 teaspoon of freshly ground black pepper and 4 eggs. Line a loaf pan with strips of bacon and pour the mixture in. Pour over this ½ cup of cognac or whisky and cover with strips of bacon. Cover and bake at 350° for 1½ to 2 hours. Remove from the oven and weight the paté down with some heavy object while it cools. When chilled, slice thin and and serve with drinks.

steak tartare

There is nothing better with drinks than a bowl of freshly ground raw beef—round or sirloin—and plenty of pumpernickel or crackers on which to spread it. Season the beef as follows: to 2 pounds of ground meat add ½ cup of finely chopped onion, 2 chopped cloves of garlic, 1 teaspoon or more of salt, 1 teaspoon of freshly ground black pepper, at least 2 tablespoons of A-1 or Worcestershire sauce and ¼ cup of chopped parsley. Mix it all together and serve in a bowl or in individual patties, with bread, crackers, butter and lots of mustard.

CHEESE

■ A big platter of a variety of good cheeses and a plate of French bread, thin-sliced rye or pumpernickel and crackers, along with some butter for those who like it, is always welcome fare with outdoor drinks.

If you have bits of cheese left in your refrigerator, you can mash them with cream cheese, flavor with a little mustard and blend well. This makes a first-class spread which can be used for the appetizer tray with crackers or toast or all kinds of vegetables. Here are some good combinations, any of which can be stored in jars in the refrigerator:

1. Blend together leftovers of Roquefort or Danish Blue cheese with cream cheese and butter and flavor with a little Worcestershire sauce and pepper. Mash the cheeses together well and flavor to taste.

2. Grind 1 pound of sharp Cheddar or store cheese (the natural, not the processed variety). Mash ¼ pound of cream cheese into it and flavor with 2 teaspoons of dry mustard, 1 tablespoon of Worcestershire sauce and 1 tablespoon or more, to taste, of chili sauce. Mix thoroughly.

3. Grind 1 pound of sharp Cheddar, mash thoroughly with ½ pound of cream cheese and combine with 1 small tin of pimentos finely cut, 2 small hot peppers, 1 teaspoon of dry mustard and enough cream or melted butter to make a good paste. Mix well with a fork.

4. Blend 1 pound of cream cheese with 1 bunch of green onions finely cut, 6-8 radishes thinly sliced, ½ cup of chopped parsley and ¼ cup of finely cut celery. Blend well with a little sweet or sour cream, salt and pepper to taste, and serve very cold with rye bread.

5. Thoroughly mash 1 large tin of French or Portuguese sardines and combine with two ¼-pound packages of cream cheese, the juice of a lemon and 1 teaspoon of finely chopped onion. Beat well with a fork until nicely blended. Add more salt if needed and 1 teaspoon of finely chopped parsley, and mix again.

Crackers and bread are the base of many appetizers. Herbs, mustard

CRACKERS
AND BREADS

Good bread and crackers are a basic ingredient of most appetizers. The salty rye bread called "icebox rye," in small loaves, is delicious when sliced thin. So are other varieties of rye and pumpernickel, especially those that are baked by the small local bakeries. French and Italian breads are excellent, and in some cities you can get the wonderful Armenian bread called *lavash*. Sliced thin, *lavash* is a fine, chewy bread for appetizers. Sourdough bread, if you can get it, is also a perfect base for appetizers.

As for crackers, you probably have your own favorites. I prefer those that don't have too strong a flavor of their own—such as sea toast and sea biscuits, Melba toast, Ry-Krisp and matzos. F.F.V. pumpernickel crackers with caraway seeds, new on the market, have a flavor that blends well with most snacks.

sliced herb bread

Take a loaf of thinly sliced sour-rye bread and spread each slice with garlic-flavored butter and sprinkle each slice with finely chopped parsley and a hint of dried thyme or rosemary. Place the slices together, loaf-fashion, wrap in foil and bake at 375° for 15 to 20 minutes or until the butter is thoroughly melted and the herb flavor is blended.

italian cheese bread

Start by spreading halves of long French or round Italian loaves lavishly with butter. Add a layer of sliced Mozzarella cheese, a layer of anchovy fillets, a layer of thinly sliced onions and a layer of chopped parsley. Press them together and heat in a 375° oven for 15 to 20 minutes. Another very satisfactory way to prepare this exceptionally tasty—and different—bread is to wrap the layers in aluminum foil and heat them on the back of the grill.

garlic bread

Rub 2 to 3 cloves of garlic well into the crust of French or Italian loaves. Heat in a 350° oven in the house or wrap in foil and heat on the back of your grill, turning often.

For mustard bread, split French loaf, hand-mix chopped onions, parsley, lemon

mustard bread

Combine ½ pound of butter with 1 cup of finely chopped green onions, ½ cup of chopped parsley and a few drops of lemon juice. Cream it well and spoon onto split halves of French or Italian bread. Top with French's Mustard and sprinkle with toasted sesame seeds. Heat on grill or—much better—in the oven, and serve hot from the kitchen.

cheese loaf

Combine ½ pound of well-softened butter, ½ pound of grated sharp Cheddar cheese, 2 teaspoons of dry mustard, a few specks of cayenne pepper and blend well. Spread or split loaves of French or Italian bread, press halves together and heat in a 375° oven until the cheese is melted, or wrap in foil and heat on the back of the grill, turning quite often while they heat.

herbed loaf

Chop a bunch of green onions or scallions, enough parsley to make ½ cup, enough fresh basil to make 2 tablespoons. Combine with ½ pound of softened butter and 1 teaspoon of dry mustard. Split 1 long French loaf or 2 round Italian loaves and, through the middle, spread with this mixture. Heat in a 375° oven for 15 minutes or wrap in foil and heat on the back part of the grill.

juice and butter. Spoon this onto the halves, top with mustard and sesame seeds

rolls

Any of these mixtures may be used with French or Italian hard rolls split and prepared the same way. This may be more advantageous for a large party.

baking-powder biscuits

Baking-powder biscuits of your own mix or made from a prepared mix are ideal for outdoor eating. Cut them larger and a little thicker than you would biscuits prepared for the dining room. Dip each one in melted butter and arrange them close together on a baking dish.

VARIATION: Top the biscuits with thinly sliced onions which have been sautéed in a small amount of butter until they are just limp. Bake as usual.

- Fold finely chopped parsley and chives into your biscuit dough and proceed as before.
- Add chopped parsley and a little thyme or sweet basil to your biscuit dough.
- Add grated Cheddar cheese and a few dashes of cayenne pepper to your biscuit dough.
- Top each biscuit with ½ lump of sugar and a tiny spoonful of orange marmalade. Dip cut biscuits in butter and roll them in sesame seeds before placing on baking sheet.

VEGETABLES
AND SALADS

are the vegetables, casseroles and salads that make barbecues inviting

Any combination of vegetables may be cooked in foil, either on the grill or in the ashes. For instance, sliced eggplant, quartered tomatoes and sliced onions, together with a bit of butter, salt and pepper, may be encased in foil and cooked.

Mushrooms may be cooked in foil with butter. Canned whole-kernel corn combined with butter, chopped green onions or chopped green pepper or grated Cheddar cheese may be wrapped in foil and broiled on the grill. It is delicious.

Whole onions or potatoes in their skins may be wrapped in foil and baked in the ashes, as can a great many other vegetables.

sautéed potatoes

Sautéed potatoes are easily prepared for outdoor eating. Slice peeled raw potatoes fairly thin and soak them in cold water for an hour or so. If you are cooking steak or roast beef, cut away some of the beef fat or get a little extra from the butcher. Cut the fat very fine, put it in a skillet (a heavy iron or cast-aluminum skillet is best) and let it melt. You will need about 1 tablespoon of suet per potato. When it is melted and the bits of suet have turned crisp, add the potato slices, after drying them on paper towels, and let them sauté gently. Turn them often with a large spatula. They should be nicely browned, crisp and cooked through. Don't break them as you turn them. Add salt and plenty of freshly ground black pepper. Potatoes cooked this way with bits of crisp suet are unbelievably good and just the thing with hearty outdoor roasts or steaks.

french fried potatoes

French fries can be soggy and unappetizing or crisp and delicious —depending on how you cook them. I have a theory that frying the potatoes twice gives a crisper product. I cut my potatoes in fairly thin strips and soak them in ice water for an hour or so. I heat the fat to 350° in a deep-fat fryer. The electric fryers have thermostats, but with the others you will need a thermometer. I dry the potatoes thoroughly on a towel and fry them in the fat until they are just faintly colored. Then I drain them well and put them on paper towels to cool. This can be done ahead of time—early in the day.

When I am ready to serve the meat course, I heat the fat again—this time to 370°—and plunge the potatoes in, a few at a time. When they are brown and crisp I serve them up piping hot. I would rather have them overcooked than undercooked. At any rate, cooking twice assures you of crisp brown French fries.

VARIATION: For Julienne or shoestring potatoes, cut the potatoes in very small matchlike strips. Fry them at 350° until they are really crisp.

potato chips

Potato chips are easy to make. Just invest in a wood cutter with diagonal blades, which you can find in a hardware shop. Take good-sized potatoes, cut them very thin and soak them in cold water for an hour or two. Dry them thoroughly on a towel. Fry them at 360° until they are lightly browned and curled. Don't fry too many at a time or they may stick together. Drain on absorbent paper and salt well.

home-fried potatoes

Start with boiled potatoes in their jackets. Peel and slice medium thin. Sauté slowly in butter or beef fat until slices are browned and crisp around the edges. Salt and pepper to taste. Turn them as they cook with a spatula, being careful not to break the slices.

hashed brown potatoes

Cut boiled potatoes into small cubes and sauté them in butter or beef fat. Press them down gently in the pan with a spatula or turner so that they will become crusty on the bottom and well browned. Turn them out on a plate or platter, keeping the brown crust on top. Be careful when you do it, or they will simply tumble into a heap. Tilt the pan gently and loosen them with the spatula. Then with a quick flip get them over and out. Season to taste just before dishing them up.

lyonnaise potatoes

Peel and chop 2 medium onions and sauté in 4 tablespoons of butter or beef fat until just soft. Add 4 or 5 good-sized boiled potatoes, peeled and sliced. Mix them with the onions. Cook slowly until the mixture is browned. Add ¼ cup of chopped parsley and salt and pepper to taste.

potatoes hashed in cream

This is a delicious, rich-tasting way to cook potatoes. Cut boiled potatoes into cubes and sauté them in butter or beef fat until they are heated through and lightly browned. Sprinkle with a little flour, salt and pepper. Gradually pour in enough heavy cream to cover the bottom of the pan and let the potatoes cook in the cream. Be careful not to let them scorch. Sprinkle liberally with paprika.

baked potatoes

It's easiest to bake the potatoes in the house and bring them out to eat with your grilled meat. I like to split them after baking, add butter, salt, pepper and paprika and blend it all together. Then I return them to the oven to heat through again.

You can bake potatoes successfully on the top of a grill, in a cast-aluminum pan tightly covered. It's a tricky job, but it can be done. You can also bake them in the coals of a dying fire, wrapped in foil.

corn

There is nothing better in the summer than freshly gathered, tender corn. Don't overcook it. Five minutes in boiling water is ample.

Broiled corn is excellent, too. Turn the husks back without tearing them off the cob, remove the long silk, dip the corn in cold water and replace the husks. Place them on the grill and let the ears roast, turning them often. Serve with plenty of butter and salt and pepper.

broiled eggplant slices

This versatile vegetable is especially good with barbecued meats.

Peel the eggplant and cut in slices ¾ of an inch thick. Dredge them lightly with flour, dot with butter and brush with oil. Broil over charcoal as you would a hamburger, turning once during the cooking. Brush again with oil after you turn them, and season to taste.

VARIATION: Sprinkle each slice with grated cheese just as you turn it.

Vegetables taste wonderful when brushed with oil or butter and grilled in foil

tomatoes

Tomatoes go wonderfully with outdoor food. In selecting tomatoes for cooking be sure they are not overripe or too juicy. Cut them in halves, flour them lightly or dip in crumbs, and broil over a low fire.

Or—and this is really more successful—sauté them in a skillet with a little butter or oil until they are just cooked through. A sprinkling of basil, either fresh or dried, or of basil seasoning powder does wonders.

fried zucchini

The small green Italian squash called zucchini makes an excellent outdoor vegetable. It cooks quickly and goes well with many foods.

Cut the zucchini, unpeeled, in very thin slices and dredge them lightly in flour. French-fry them in fat heated to 365° until they are crisp and cooked through—about 5 minutes. Drain and season.

sautéed zucchini

This dish can be prepared quickly on top of the grill. Cut 6 small zucchini in quarters without peeling them. Heat 5 tablespoons of olive oil in an iron skillet. Add the zucchini and 2 cloves of shredded garlic. Sauté lightly for 5 to 8 minutes, turning frequently with a spatula. Cover the pan and cook for 2 or 3 minutes more. Season to taste.

The Borden Company

CASSEROLES

■ Some of the food you eat out of doors will have to be cooked indoors, which means that kitchen duty will have to be done. If you are planning a beach or picnic barbecue that will take you far from home, however, do not feel that you must rule these tasty side dishes off your menu. Insulated bags and boxes will bring your kitchen-made casseroles piping hot to the barbecue site.

lima-bean casserole

Sauté 2 finely chopped garlic cloves and 6 to 8 finely cut green onions in ¼ cup of olive oil. Add 4 medium tomatoes, peeled, squeezed to remove the seeds and finely chopped. Add 1 teaspoon of basil, 1 of salt and 1 of freshly ground black pepper and let it all cook slowly for 20 minutes. Add 1 small can of tomato sauce, bring it to a boil and cook for 5 minutes. Pour this sauce over the contents of 2 packages of quick-frozen lima beans which have been cooked according to the directions on the package, and blend well. Pour into an oiled casserole. Dot with butter and sprinkle with grated Romano or Parmesan cheese and bake at 350° for 20 to 25 minutes.

summer-vegetable casserole

Combine 1 cup each French-style string beans (cut lengthwise), fresh, canned or frozen green peas; fresh, canned or frozen whole-kernel corn and fresh or canned tiny cooked onions. Prepare a rich cream sauce with 4 tablespoons of butter, 3 tablespoons of flour. Cook together until well blended. Gradually stir in 1 cup of heavy cream. Continue stirring until well thickened. Add ½ cup grated Cheddar or imported Swiss cheese. Add salt and pepper to taste, 1 teaspoon of dry mustard and a dash of Worcestershire sauce. Stir until cheese is melted, then pour over the cooked vegetables. Sprinkle with grated Parmesan cheese. Cover and bake at 350° until the vegetables are thoroughly reheated and blended with the sauce.

baked beans

Clementine Paddleford of the New York *Herald Tribune* wrote the other day that she would have been amazed to see anyone open a can of pork and beans at a picnic when she was a child. I would have been amazed, too, for we always brought along a huge pan of home-made baked beans, made with salt pork, onion and mustard and a very little brown sugar. Too much sweet spoils the flavor of baked beans, to my mind. My mother's baked beans were famous all over the beach colony. Here is how she made them:

Soak a pint of white pea beans overnight. In the morning put them to cook in salted water—more than enough to cover them. Add an onion stuck with 2 cloves and a bay leaf. Let the beans simmer until soft but not mushy. Drain them and save the cooking water. Place a layer of beans in a large casserole, cover it with thin slices of salt pork and onion, add another layer of beans, and sprinkle it with dry mustard. Now add a layer of garlic sausage, salami or summer sausage, another layer of sliced onions, more dry mustard and just a sprinkling of brown sugar. Top with a layer of beans and cover with slices of salt pork. Pour the liquid from cooking the beans over this and bake it at 300° for 2 or 3 hours, adding more water if it gets too dry.

black-bean casserole

Soak 2 pounds of black beans overnight. Pour this water off the next morning and cover to 1 inch above beans with fresh water. Add 1 onion stuck with 2 cloves, a bay leaf and 2 garlic cloves and cook until the beans are tender. Remove the beans to a casserole, strain the liquid and combine with ½ cup of dark rum and ½ cup of tomato purée. Pour this over the beans and top with thin slices of salt pork which have been parboiled for 30 minutes. Bake at 350° until the salt pork is nicely browned and cooked through and the beans well blended. Serve with pork dishes and with such game dishes as duck and pheasant.

string beans and mushrooms

Split 1½ pounds of tender green beans lengthwise and cook in a small amount of boiling salted water until they are just tender. Drain, sauté ½ pound of sliced mushrooms in ¼ pound of butter until heated through, add the beans and cook very quickly. Remove to a casserole, sprinkle with grated Parmesan cheese. Dot with butter and bake at 350° for 15 minutes.

mexican fried beans

This dish—frijoles—is a mainstay of the Mexican menu and a delicious addition to your barbecue-cooking repertory. Since beans have about as much protein as meat, you can serve frijoles as a hearty main dish, with a salad on the side. It's a good dish to make in quantity for a large crowd—or to store and serve again as *frijoles refritos*—refried beans. Here's how: Wash a pint or more of pink beans (if you can't get them, use pinto beans). Put them on to cook with 2 quarts of water and an onion stuck with 2 cloves. Add a tablespoon of salt and let them cook until soft but not mushy (test them now and then while cooking). In a heavy pot, put about ⅓ pound of lard (for the authentic Mexican flavor) or bacon or chicken fat if you prefer. When it is melted add some of the beans and mash them down well. Then add some of the bean liquor and repeat this process until all the beans are used up.

Don't mash as thoroughly as you would potatoes; leave some of the beans whole and others mashed. Serve as is, thick and delectable.

For *frijoles refritos* you simply heat some fat in your skillet and fry the beans again, crushing and stirring them and letting them get really crusty and wonderful.

sauteed corn

Sauté two finely chopped garlic cloves in ¼ cup of olive oil. Add 2 cans of whole-kernel corn and toss well until the corn is thoroughly heated. Add ⅓ cup of heavy cream and sprinkle lavishly with fresh grated Parmesan or Romano cheese and allow it to simmer for 3 to 4 minutes before serving.

corn casserole

Butter a 2-quart casserole. Add ¼ cup of finely chopped green onions, ¼ cup of finely chopped green peppers which have been sautéed in ¼ cup of olive oil for 5 minutes. Blend with 2 small cans of whole-kernel corn, ½ cup of grated, imported Swiss cheese, ½ cup of heavy cream. Dot with butter, sprinkle with sesame seeds, cover and bake at 350° for 20 to 25 minutes.

onion casserole

Slice 6 medium to large-sized onions in rather thick slices. Place in a well-buttered casserole and cover with beef bouillon or consommé. The canned bouillon or consommé works perfectly for this recipe. Cover and bake at 350° for approximately 20 minutes. Add ½ cup of coarsely grated Cheddar or imported Swiss cheese and return to oven for 5 to 7 minutes before serving.

risi pisi

Cook 1½ cups of your favorite rice in your favorite marinade. Drain and combine with 2 tins of tiny French peas, which have been heated in their own juice, drained and combined with ½ cup or more of melted butter. Toss them well together, sprinkle with a little finely chopped parsley and serve.

other rice combinations

These recipes are all based on 1½ cups of rice before it is cooked in your preferred manner.

1. Combine cooked rice with ½ cup of finely chopped parsley, ¼ cup of finely chopped chives and ⅓ cup of melted butter.

2. Combine rice with 1 cup of finely chopped green onions which have been sautéed with ¼ pound of butter. Salt and pepper to taste. Sprinkle with chopped parsley.

3. Cook the rice with a small pinch of saffron and use beef broth or consommé instead of water. Combine the cooked rice with ½ cup of melted butter and ⅓ cup of grated Romano or Parmesan cheese. Toss lightly and sprinkle lavishly with chopped parsley.

4. Combine cooked rice with 1 cup of finely chopped mushrooms which have been sautéed in ½ cup of butter and seasoned well with salt, pepper and a dash of Worcestershire sauce.

5. Combine 3 cups of cooked rice—this is the equivalent of 1½ cups of uncooked rice—with 1 cup of grated (imported) Swiss cheese and 1 cup of sour cream. Toss the ingredients together over low heat until the cheese is melted and the cream is heated through, but do not allow them to come to a boil. Salt and pepper to taste.

baked eggplant

Cut 1 large or 2 medium-sized eggplants into ½-inch slices. Dip the the slices into seasoned flour and brown lightly in olive oil. Slice 6 peeled ripe tomatoes, 3 large onions and 3 green peppers. Alternate slices of eggplant with sliced onions, tomatoes and peppers, dotting each layer with butter and sprinkling with Parmesan cheese: salt and pepper to taste. Make the top layer eggplant and over it pour ⅓ cup of olive oil, sprinkle with bread crumbs and grated Parmesan cheese. Cover and bake at 375° for 1½ to 2 minutes.

ratatouille

⅓ cup olive oil	3 medium-sized zucchini
1 eggplant diced	(cut in slices but not peeled)
Flour	1 large onion, finely chopped
1 clove garlic, chopped	3 tomatoes, peeled and cut in
Basil or oregano	slices

Heat the olive oil in a large skillet. Dredge the zucchini slices and the eggplant lightly with flour and sauté in the oil until tender and nicely browned. Add the finely chopped onion and garlic and continue cooking until soft and well blended with the eggplant and zucchini. Lastly add the tomatoes and let it all cook over a brisk heat for 10 to 15 minutes or until it is well mixed and has the appearance of a vegetable stew—which it is. Salt and pepper to taste (adding a pinch of basil or oregano) and transfer to an oval or round baking dish which may be used for serving.

The quantities in this recipe may be increased and the dish is equally delicious when served cold with additional oil to which a dash of orange or lemon juice has been added. In this case it is pleasant to combine it with black olives and sautéed mushrooms.

United Fresh Fruit and Vegetable Association

SALADS

raw vegetable bowl

Either for an appetizer or a side dish, I like raw vegetables with plain salt and pepper, or with a dunking sauce. I like to use endive, celery, cucumber, onions and pickles. They should all be thoroughly iced and crisp. Salt and pepper is really all you need, but if you want a dressing, make it a separate bowl of highly seasoned mayonnaise into which the greens can be dunked.

To season mayonnaise for this, add chopped garlic, onion, hard-cooked egg, capers and a touch of tomato.

If you are serving a Sunday breakfast party, try radishes crisp and cold with a little butter. This is a French and German idea; you'll have to try it to see how good it is.

potato salad

Of the many versions of this famous salad, here is my favorite:

Boil 6 to 8 medium-sized potatoes in their jackets until just barely done. While they are still hot, peel them and slice them into a bowl. You can manage the hot potatoes with a fork and a little cold running water. Heat 1 cup of olive or peanut oil, ⅓ cup of red wine vinegar, 1 teaspoon of salt and 1 teaspoon of freshly ground black pepper in a pan. When it reaches the boiling point pour it over the potato slices. Add ½ teaspoon of celery seed and ½ teaspoon of mustard seed and let the potatoes cool. Cover and chill until you are ready to use. Before serving, add ½ cup of finely chopped raw onion and ¼ cup of finely chopped parsley. Add more oil and vinegar if necessary. Taste for seasoning.

green salad

Green salad is standard at most outdoor parties. It goes very well with beefsteak or hearty hamburgers. Be sure your greens are crisp and dry. Water dilutes the dressing. Get a salad basket into which you can put the greens to shake off all the water, or dry them by wrapping loosely in a clean towel and shaking.

Break your greens in bite-size pieces into your bowl. Make a dressing of four parts oil to one part wine vinegar or lemon juice. I prefer the latter. Add salt and freshly ground black pepper to taste and any seasonings you like, such as mustard, garlic, herbs, Worcestershire, or Angostura bitters. Pour the dressing over the greens and toss at the

Old London

last minute. Tossing should be done thoroughly. Dig down to the bottom of the bowl with your fork and spoon and bring each piece of green up to the top so that all the salad gets a good coating of dressing.

VARIATION: For a Caesar salad, sprinkle a little grated Italian cheese —Parmesan or Romano—into the dressing, add a few chopped anchovies, some croutons (squares of bread cooked in olive oil and garlic until crisp) and a raw egg. Mix this thoroughly and pour over the greens. It's very filling, so don't serve it with a heavy meal.

- Add quartered tomatoes, sliced cucumbers and sliced radishes to the greens. This is a chiffonade salad.
- Add cooked green beans and green peas to the greens, toss the salad and top with thin raw-onion rings. This is very good with chicken.
- Add a few chilled shrimp to the salad.
- Add hunks of crabmeat.
- Add bits of crisp bacon for a delicate touch.

cucumber salad

Peel two good-sized cucumbers and split them in half. With a spoon, scrape out the seeds and throw them away. Slice the cucumber shells very thin. Place them in a bowl and season with salt. Cover with equal parts of mayonnaise and sour cream and chill for 2 or 3 hours.

VARIATION: Add finely chopped fresh dill to the dressing.
- Add chopped chives or green onions to the dressing.
- Add chopped tarragon to the dressing.

cole slaw

This hearty salad is ideal for outdoor eating. It can be made well in advance, as it mellows with sitting awhile.

For 6 servings, shred a large, firm head of white or red cabbage very fine. Wash it and dry it well, place it in a large bowl and pour over it the following dressing. Blend together 1 cup of sour cream, sweet cream or buttermilk, ¼ cup of oil, 3 tablespoons of sugar (or more, according to taste), ¼ cup of red wine vinegar, ½ teaspoon of celery seeds, ½ teaspoon of mustard seeds, and salt to taste. Toss the salad well and let it stand in a cold place at least an hour or two before eating. Vary the sugar and the cream in the dressing to suit your own taste.

VARIATION: Make a dressing of 1 cup of sour cream, the juice of a lemon, 1 tablespoon of sugar, 1 teaspoon of dry mustard and 1 tablespoon of horse-radish. Thin down with a little water if necessary. Salt to taste.

VARIATION: Combine the cabbage with 1 cup of mayonnaise, ½ cup of sour cream, the juice of a lemon, 1 tablespoon of sugar and ½ teaspoon each of celery seed and mustard seed. Salt and pepper to taste.

Sauce adds the fillip to many a meat; the dressing decides the fate

SAUCES AND MARINADES

of the salad. What shall it be—forthright or subtle, piquant or bland?

When it comes to sauces, most dyed-in-the-wool barbecuers like to express their own individualities. This is all to the good, provided you don't mix ingredients whose flavors conflict. There are certain classical combinations that have stood the test of time, and these with a bit of variation answer all purposes. Here are proven recipes for all of the basic sauces and dressings for meats, vegetables and salads.

A good thing to keep in mind when cooking any sauce is that if it seems too thin at the end of the given cooking period, you can always reduce it and thicken it by cooking it over high heat, with the cover off, until it reaches the desired consistency.

For dishes that should be marinated a long time—such as shish kebab —put the cubes of meat in a jar with a lid. Cover them with the marinade and put the lid on. Then if you do not use all of the meat, you can leave it in the jar in the sauce and keep it in the refrigerator.

SAUCES

simple steak sauce

Chop enough shallots, green onions or scallions to make 1½ cups. Melt ¼ pound of butter in a skillet and add the onions or shallots. Do not sauté them—merely let them blend together and wilt down. Add 1 teaspoon of salt and 1 cup of white wine and bring it to a boil. Lower the heat and simmer for 5 minutes. Add ¼ cup of chopped parsley and another chunk of butter. Boil for 3 minutes, add some freshly ground black pepper and taste for seasoning. Serve with steak or any broiled or roasted meat. I'm sure you'll find this blend of flavors unique and satisfying—and it's an easy sauce to make.

VARIATION: Add 3 tablespoons of finely chopped anchovies just before removing the sauce from the heat. Blend thoroughly.

VARIATION: Use 2 cups of chopped shallots or green onions. Add 1 tablespoon of fresh or 1½ teaspoons of dried tarragon. Substitute red wine for the white and add a dash of vinegar.

creole steak sauce

Mix in a skillet ½ pound of butter, 1 cup of catsup, ½ cup of Worcestershire sauce, 1 onion stuck with 3 cloves, 2 cloves of garlic, 1 cup of consommé, 1 tablespoon of prepared mustard, 1 teaspoon of salt and ½ teaspoon of freshly ground black pepper. Bring to a boil and simmer for 30 minutes. Remove it from the fire and put the sauce through a food mill or mix it in an electric blender. Return it to the skillet and simmer it again for 10 minutes. This sauce will keep in the refrigerator or it may be deep-frozen for longer storage.

devil sauce

Heat 5 or 6 tablespoons of butter in a skillet. Sauté 3 cloves of garlic finely chopped and 1 medium onion finely chopped until they are just soft. Add ¼ cup of chopped pickle, 2 tablespoons of vinegar, ½ cup of catsup and ½ cup of Worcestershire sauce. Bring to a boil and add 1 teaspoon of salt, 1 teaspoon of dry mustard, a dash or two of Tabasco sauce and a few capers. Serve with any meat or poultry dish calling for a deviled sauce or a pungent sauce. If you like a thicker sauce, add small balls of flour and butter kneaded together and stir until the sauce is thickened and smooth.

uncooked barbecue sauce

Nothing could be simpler than this sauce. It can be shaken in a cocktail shaker or mixed in an electric blender. Combine the following: 2 crushed cloves of garlic, 1½ teaspoons of salt, 1 teaspoon of freshly ground or crushed black pepper, or ¼ cup of finely sliced scallions or green onions, 2 teaspoons of prepared mustard, 1 teaspoon of dry mustard, the juice of 1 lemon, ⅓ cup of A-1 or Heinz Beefsteak Sauce and 2 cups of tomato sauce, tomato purée or strained canned tomatoes. Shake furiously, add a dash of Tabasco if you wish, and taste for seasoning. If it seems a little too sharp, add a touch of brown sugar.

basic barbecue sauce

Here is a basic sauce that you can vary in as many ways as your imagination and taste suggest. Peel and chop 5 to 7 cloves of garlic and press into 2 teaspoons of coarse salt. Add 2 finely chopped onions. Heat 1 cup of olive or peanut oil in a skillet, add the garlic and onions and let them wilt down and blend thoroughly. When they are soft, add 1 cup of tomato sauce or strained canned tomatoes, 1 cup of Worcestershire sauce, 1 cup of red wine vinegar and ½ cup of brown sugar or honey. Season with 1 teaspoon of rosemary or rosemary seasoning powder, ½ teaspoon of thyme, 3 tablespoons of chopped green pepper and ¼ cup of chopped parsley. Bring to a boil, lower the heat and simmer for 20 minutes. Taste for seasoning. You may strain it if you wish, or put it in an electric blender to get a smoother mixture. Use this sauce hot or cold with either meat or fish. Baste with it and serve with the finished dish.

VARIATION: Mexican. Add 3 tablespoons of chili powder and a few finely chopped hot chilies to the sauce before cooking. Add a few dashes of Tabasco if you like it extra hot.

- Italian: Omit the Worcestershire sauce and the vinegar. Add 1 cup of tomato purée, 1 tablespoon of fresh or 1 teaspoon of dried basil, a pinch of oregano, 1 cup of red wine. You may add 1 cup of consommé if you wish.
- Californian: Omit the vinegar and sugar. Add 1 cup of red wine, ½ cup of orange juice, the grated rind of an orange, the juice of 1 lemon and 1 cup of finely chopped ripe olives.
- Tabasco: Combine 1 cup of vinegar, 1 clove of crushed garlic, 2 tablespoons Worcestershire, 1 teaspoon of dry mustard, ½ teaspoon of Tabasco, 1 tablespoon of sugar, ½ cup of catsup, 1 teaspoon of salt. Combine ingredients and simmer 10 minutes. Brush chicken, spareribs or other meats with this sauce before broiling and baste with it during cooking, and serve as a sauce with the finished dish.

pungent barbecue sauce

Peel and chop 6 cloves of garlic and sauté them in 1 cup of peanut or olive oil until browned and almost crisp. Add 1 cup of finely chopped onion or shallot and cook until just wilted and soft but not brown. Add 1 cup of finely chopped green pepper, 1 cup of finely chopped peeled and seeded tomato and 1 or 2 stalks of celery finely chopped. Season with 1 tablespoon of basil, 1 tablespoon of chili powder and ¼ cup of chopped parsley. Pour over this 1 cup of red wine, 1 cup of consommé or 1 cup of water to which you have added 2 bouillon cubes and 1 tablespoon of vinegar. Cover and simmer for about 40 minutes. Put the sauce through a strainer or blend it in an electric blender. Add 1 cup of tomato purée, 1½ teaspoons of salt, 1 teaspoon of freshly ground black pepper and simmer again for 10 minutes. The longer this sauce simmers the better it is. It may be used either hot or cold for basting or serving with meats or fish.

mexican barbecue sauce

Melt 6 tablespoons of shortening (bacon fat or margarine will do nicely) and add 3 large onions finely chopped and 2 cloves of garlic finely chopped. Sauté until just soft. Add 1 pound of chopped beef and mix well. Sauté for 4 or 5 minutes. Add 2 tablespoons of chili powder, 1 teaspoon of cumin and 1 bay leaf crumbled. Cover with consommé or water and simmer until well blended and thickened. Salt to taste and add a dash of Tabasco if you like. Serve this sauce over frankfurters or hamburgers with finely chopped raw onions and ripe olives. It is also a superb sauce for rice or spaghetti.

mexican barbecue sauce no. 2

This sauce is useful for many different dishes and is especially good for barbecuing turkey or chicken. Soak 6 to 8 chili peppers in water for several hours. Remove the skins and force the peppers through the food mill. Soak 2 or 3 hot peppers, remove the seeds and chop the peppers very fine. Combine with the chilies and add 2 or 3 pimentos.

Sauté 3 large onions, finely chopped, in 6 tablespoons of fat until they are just soft. Add the pepper mixture, 2 cups of chicken broth and 1 can of green molé sauce and cook it all down for 1 or 2 hours. Correct the seasoning. This sauce is better made the day before so that it will mellow overnight. I like to add 1 can of tomato purée and about ½ cup of white or red wine and ¼ cup of chopped almonds. (See "Sources of Supply" for places where you can get canned molé sauce and other Mexican specialties.)

If you serve a barbecued turkey with this sauce, have this wonderful Mexican bean dish with it: Cook up some black or kidney beans. Then toss them in a skillet with plenty of fat or butter, season them with garlic and mash them down to a paste. Put a large glob of sour cream on each portion.

california barbecue sauce

For an excellent barbecue sauce for beef or pork, use the following ingredients:

1 onion, chopped fine	1 tablespoon Worcestershire
1 clove garlic, minced	¼ cup brown sugar
1 teaspoon salt	¼ cup vinegar
⅛ teaspoon pepper	1 can tomato sauce
½ teaspoon chili powder	1 can tomato purée
½ teaspoon celery salt	1 slice lemon
½ teaspoon dry mustard	⅛ teaspoon Tabasco

Combine ingredients in your skillet or saucepan in order listed, over medium heat. Cover and simmer for about 20 minutes, or until sauce reaches desired consistency.

salsa fria

This is a famous Mexican sauce which I find can be used for many barbecue dishes. It's simple to make and can easily be added to.

Peel, seed and chop 2 to 2½ pounds of ripe tomatoes. If you can't get good fresh home-grown tomatoes, use a No. 2½ can of solid-pack tomatoes and chop them up. Combine with chopped fresh or dried hot pepper—as much as you think you will like, finely chopped. Add 1 teaspoon of salt, 1 teaspoon of freshly ground or cracked black pepper, 1 large onion finely chopped, a clove of chopped garlic, 2 tablespoons of lemon juice or vinegar and ¼ cup of olive oil. Blend well and chill. Serve with grilled food or almost any meat or fish dish.

VARIATION: Add finely chopped green pepper.

• Buy canned plum tomatoes, Italian style, chop and add to the sauce.

• Add cucumbers, finely chopped.

• If you like a really hot sauce, add more hot peppers.

chinese barbecue sauce

This simple sauce is powerful and pungent—the best for marinating Chinese barbecue dishes. Mix together 1 cup of soy sauce, 1 teaspoon of monosodium glutamate, 2 or 3 cloves of garlic finely chopped, 1 tablespoon of grated fresh ginger or chopped dried ginger and ½ cup of sherry. Use it for a marinade and for basting.

chinese sweet-and-sour sauce

Combine in a skillet ½ cup of wine vinegar, ½ cup of water, 1 cup of sugar, 2 tablespoons of soy sauce, ½ cup of white wine or sherry, 1 cup of pineapple chunks, 3 or 4 green onions cut in strips, 1 large green pepper cut in strips and 3 large tomatoes cut in wedges. Bring to a boil. Mix 1½ tablespoons of cornstarch with a little vinegar and water. Stir slowly into the sauce until it thickens. Taste for seasoning and serve with any dish calling for sweet-sour sauce.

SERVING SAUCES

creole sauce

Sauté in ¼ pound of butter 1 large onion, 2 cloves of garlic, 2 green peppers and 2 stalks of celery all coarsely chopped. After the vegetables have cooked for 5 minutes, add ½ cup of sherry, cover the pan and simmer for 20 minutes. Add 1 No. 2½ can of solid-pack tomatoes chopped, 1½ cups of tomato juice, 1 teaspoon of salt, 1 teaspoon of freshly ground pepper, 1 teaspoon of thyme or oregano, ½ cup of brown sugar and 3 tablespoons of vinegar. Simmer for 30 minutes and taste for seasoning. This sauce can be served with any Creole-style meat or fish dish.

VARIATION: Many people like the addition of gumbo filé (powdered okra) and a few pieces of whole okra. Canned okra is generally available; for the Louisiana flavoring, gumbo filé, try the specialty groceries or mail-order suppliers (see "Sources of Supply").

italian sauce

This delicious sauce for hamburgers or spaghetti is no cinch to make, but the results are well worth the time and effort. Heat ½ cup of olive oil in a big skillet. Add 1 large can of small Italian plum tomatoes or 2 pounds of fresh plum tomatoes split in two. Add 1 tablespoon of basil and 1 teaspoon of salt and simmer slowly for 1½ hours. Strain through a fine sieve. While the tomatoes are simmering, sauté 1 pound of ground beef and ½ pound of ground pork in 4 tablespoons of beef fat or olive oil. Add 3 cloves of garlic finely chopped, ½ teaspoon of thyme, ½ cup of ripe olives pitted and chopped, ¼ cup of finely chopped green pepper, 1 teaspoon of salt, 1 teaspoon of freshly ground black pepper and 1 cup of red wine. Simmer for 30 minutes. Combine this with the tomato sauce and let the whole mixture simmer for another 30 minutes. Taste for seasoning. Serve this sauce with spaghetti, noodles, meats, poultry, or use it as a basting sauce. When you use it as sauce for spaghetti or noodles, serve plenty of grated Parmesan or Romano cheese with it.

VARIATION: If you like your sauce with a stronger tomato flavor, add a tin of Italian tomato purée during the last 20 minutes of cooking.

- You can turn this into a delicious chili sauce by adding 2 tablespoons of chili powder or some of the canned, prepared chili sauce sold in Mexican stores, in a quantity to suit your taste.
- You can make a substitute Chinese curry sauce by adding 4 tablespoons of soy sauce, 3 tablespoons of fresh ginger finely chopped and 1 to 2 tablespoons of curry powder, according to your taste. This is delicious served with barbecued shrimp, barbecued lamb or beef.

anchovy butter sauce

Melt 6 tablespoons of butter in a small skillet, add 1 or more tablespoons of anchovy paste or crush several anchovy fillets in the butter. Add a few drops of lemon juice and serve with fish or steak.

tabasco butter

Mix together ½ cup of butter or margarine, ½ teaspoon of salt, the juice of ½ lemon, 1 teaspoon of chopped parsley (optional) and ¼ teaspoon of Tabasco. Stir to a creamy consistency, chill and serve with broiled fish.

hollandaise sauce

Cut ¼ pound of butter into 3 parts. Place one piece in the upper part of a double boiler with 3 egg yolks. Put over hot, but not boiling, water and beat constantly with a wire whisk. As the butter melts, add another piece until all the butter is beaten into the egg yolks. Never let the water boil. Beat until the sauce thickens, add salt to taste and season with the juice of a lemon or 1 tablespoon of tarragon vinegar. If the sauce curdles, add a little boiling water, a few drops at a time, until the sauce smooths out again.

VARIATION: Add ½ teaspoon of dry mustard to the sauce.

- This sauce can be made much more easily and quickly in your Blendor. In a small saucepan heat 1 stick of butter to bubbling, but do not let it brown. Into the container of the Blendor put 3 egg yolks, 2 tablespoons of lemon juice, ¼ teaspoon of salt and a pinch of cayenne. Cover container and flick motor quickly on and off high speed. Remove cover, turn motor on high and gradually add the hot butter. Makes ¾ cup, or enough for 4 servings. Serve it on cooked broccoli, asparagus, cauliflower or poached eggs.

béarnaise sauce

Put 3 shallots or onions, a sprig of parsley, a sprig of tarragon (or a pinch of dried tarragon) and a sprig of chervil (or a pinch of dried chervil) in a pan with 4 to 5 tablespoons of wine vinegar and half as much water. Bring to a boil and boil for several minutes. Put through a strainer. Put 4 egg yolks in the upper part of a double boiler and place over hot, but not boiling, water. Gradually add the strained liquid, beating constantly with a wire whisk. When the sauce has thickened, add 4 tablespoons of softened butter, one at a time, and blend thoroughly. Season with salt to taste and a dash of cayenne.

VARIATION: Chopped parsley and a bit of tarragon make an interesting addition to this sauce.

- Béarnaise sauce can also be made in the Blendor. In a skillet combine 2 tablespoons of white wine, 1 tablespoon of tarragon vinegar, 2 teaspoons of chopped fresh tarragon or 1 teaspoon of dried tarragon, 2 teaspoons of chopped shallots or onion and ¼ teaspoon of freshly ground black pepper. Bring liquid to a boil and cook rapidly until almost all of it evaporates. Pour remaining mixture into the hollandaise sauce as made in the Blendor (recipe above), cover and blend on high speed for 4 seconds. Serve on broiled meats.

mayonnaise

There are several secrets to making good mayonnaise. First, use only good olive oil and the best fresh eggs. Second, have all ingredients at room temperature. And third, add the oil very slowly.

Select a shallow dish and use a silver fork for mixing. Start with 2 egg yolks, add salt to taste and a bit of dry mustard. Blend them thoroughly with the fork and then start adding the olive oil, beating thoroughly all the time. You will need about 1 cup of oil. If it starts to curdle, start another batch with 1 egg yolk and some oil and gradually stir in the curdled mixture. If the dressing seems to be getting too thick, add a few drops of lemon juice or vinegar. Continue adding the oil and beating until all the oil is used up. Taste for seasoning. You may want to add more salt, lemon juice or vinegar, or perhaps some cayenne.

remoulade sauce

To 1 cup of mayonnaise add 1 teaspoon of dry mustard, 1 tablespoon of anchovies finely chopped, 1 tablespoon of chopped parsley, 1 clove of garlic grated, some capers and chopped hard-cooked egg, a bit of tarragon and chopped olives if you like. Some people like to add horse-radish and chopped green pepper, too.

russian dressing

To mayonnaise add chili sauce, chopped onion, chopped olives and chopped hard-cooked egg to taste.

green mayonnaise

To mayonnaise add finely chopped parsley, spinach, chives, tarragon and chervil. Flavor with a little grated garlic.

tuna mayonnaise

To mayonnaise add 1 small can of tuna, mashed, 2 or 3 anchovies, also mashed, and a dash of lemon juice.

MARINADES

tenderizing marinade

This is one of my favorites. Soak tough pieces of meat in this for 6 to 24 hours before barbecuing and see if you don't have delicious results. Combine ½ cup of olive or vegetable oil, ½ cup of soy sauce and ½ cup of bourbon whisky. Add 2 small onions thinly sliced, 2 chopped cloves of garlic and 3 tablespoons of chopped fresh or preserved ginger. Add 1 teaspoon of freshly ground black pepper, 1 teaspoon of dry mustard and a touch of wine vinegar. Use for basting as well.

shish kebab marinade no. 1

One cup of red wine, ½ cup of soy sauce, 1 cup of orange or pineapple juice, 1 teaspoon of thyme, 1 teaspoon of rosemary seasoning powder, ¼ cup of Worcestershire sauce, 1 cup of finely chopped onion and 1 teaspoon of freshly ground black pepper.

shish kebab marinade no. 2

Three cloves of garlic crushed and rubbed into 1 tablespoon of coarse salt, 1 cup of sweet sherry, 1 cup of orange juice, 2 tablespoons of vinegar, 1 tablespoon of basil, 1 teaspoon of rosemary seasoning powder, ¼ cup of chopped parsley, ½ cup of Worcestershire sauce and ¼ cup of brown sugar or honey.

shish kebab marinade no. 3

One cup of soy sauce, 1 cup of pineapple juice, 1 cup of pineapple cubes, 1 cup of port or sherry, 6 cloves of garlic crushed, 1 tablespoon of tarragon leaves or tarragon seasoning powder and 1 tablespoon of freshly ground black pepper.

javanese marinade

Combine 1 cup of soy sauce, 1 cup of sesame or peanut oil, 1 cup of chopped onion or shallots, 3 tablespoons of grated ginger (fresh or candied), Chinese parsley or coriander seeds, curry powder to taste (depending on how hot you like it) and a pinch of cumin.

VARIATION: Use half curry powder and half chili powder. Or add 1 cup of brown sugar and 1 cup of white wine to the marinade. This gives it an unusual flavor.

hibachi marinade no. 1

Blend together ½ cup of soy sauce, 2 garlic cloves chopped, 2 table-spoons of grated fresh ginger (or substitute candied ginger from which you have washed the sugar), ¼ cup of brown sugar and ½ cup of sherry (which most nearly resembles the oriental wines used by the Japanese).

hibachi marinade no. 2

Add to the above: curry powder to taste, monosodium glutamate and a little chopped green onion or Chinese parsley (sometimes known as cilantro or fresh coriander; shop for it in Chinese, Mexican or Puerto Rican districts).

marinade for game and stew meat

Mix together 2 cups of red wine, the juice of 1 orange and 2 lemons, 1 large onion peeled and sliced, 8 crushed peppercorns, a spring of thyme, 1 teaspoon of oregano, 2 carrots cut in quarters, a few celery leaves, 1 bay leaf, 2 cloves of garlic chopped, ¼ cup of wine vinegar and ½ cup of olive or peanut oil; salt to taste.

VARIATION: If you like the Chinese style of flavoring, add 1 cup of soy sauce and 4 teaspoons of finely chopped fresh ginger.
• If you like curry, add 2 tablespoons of curry powder.
• If you want an extra fine marinade, rub the meat with cognac, place in a large pan and blaze it with ½ cup of warmed cognac and then pour your marinade over it.

111

To top off a barbecue, a light dessert is just the ticket—fresh fruit

DESSERTS

or ice cream. Don't forget that all-important pot of fragrant coffee

When you've had a hearty outdoors meal, you probably won't want a heavy dessert. Since most outdoor cooking takes place in the summer, you can take advantage of the abundance of good fresh fruit on the market. Frozen fruits may be substituted for fresh in many of the suggestions that follow.

Ice cream, of course, is a traditional dessert for outdoor meals, and at the end of this chapter you'll find a list of both fresh and cooked fruits that make admirable toppings.

strawberries jamaica
Hull 1 quart of strawberries and cover them with slightly sweetened pineapple juice. Let them stand for 1 hour and add rum to taste—about ¼ cup. Top with 1½ cups of heavy cream whipped with 2 tablespoons of sugar and a few drops of vanilla. Serve at once.

strawberry short toast a la helen brown
This is an ideal outdoor dish. Toast slices of good home-made bread and butter them heavily. Cover with sweetened strawberries and serve with heavy cream, whipped or plain. I think you'll find this variation a welcome change from doughy shortcake.

strawberries and cognac
Stem fresh strawberries and cut them in halves. Sprinkle liberally with sugar and add ½ cup of cognac for each quart of berries. Let them stand in a cool place for at least an hour before serving.

strawberries romanoff
Hull a quart of strawberries and arrange them in a serving bowl. Sprinkle them with 4 tablespoons of sugar, ½ cup of orange juice and ½ cup of port or sherry. Let them stand for an hour and then mix them with 1½ cups of heavy cream whipped and flavored with a little Grand Marnier or Cointreau. (You can buy small individual bottles of these liqueurs in most liquor stores.) Serve as soon as the cream is mixed in. This dessert has real elegance.

raspberries

1. Really ripe red raspberries are so good that they need nothing but the addition of a little heavy sweet cream or sour cream.

2. Raspberries with Kirsch: Kirsch is a cherry brandy made in France, Germany and in the state of Oregon. It is particularly good with all kinds of fruits. Merely a little sugar and a dash of kirsch turns a simple fruit dessert into a glamorous dish. Try it on raspberries.

3. Raspberries and Pineapple: This is a wonderful combination. If you use frozen raspberries, let them thaw out over the pineapple— canned, fresh or frozen. Add a dash of kirsch or cognac if you like.

blueberries

Large ripe blueberries, chilled and served with maple syrup and sour cream, is a delicious and refreshing dessert.

bananas

1. Select firm bananas, and slit each one through the skin down one side. Do not peel. Put them on the grill and broil them in their skins until they are charred and soft to the touch. Using tongs, remove them to individual plates. Pass rum, sugar and lemon wedges and let each guest season his own.

2. Peel firm bananas and rub with sugar. Arrange on the grill and sprinkle with lemon juice. Broil until just delicately browned but not mushy. Transfer them to a flameproof platter, add another sprinkling of sugar and pour ¼ cup of rum over them. Ignite the rum and carry blazing to the table.

watermelon

1. Choose a large ripe watermelon and cut a top slice off the long way, about ⅓ of the way down. Remove the melon meat down to the last layer of pink, scooping it out so that the shell of the bottom section of melon will form a big bowl. Cut the melon meat into cubes or into balls with a ball cutter. Add any other fruit you like to it—apricots, pineapple, strawberries, oranges, practically any fresh fruit will do— and mix it all together. Heap the fruit back into the shell until it is piled high. Add cognac or kirsch and chill melon well before serving.

2. Watermelon Supreme: This is a dish my mother used to serve frequently during the warm summer months, and it was a great delight to all of us. Plug a fine ripe watermelon and pour in as much champagne as it will hold. Replace the plug and cover it with Scotch tape. Cover the melon completely with ice. Or you can put it in your refrigerator if you have the space for it. Let it chill for at least 12 hours—24 hours is even better. Your guests will remember this dish for a long time.

other melons

Any kind of melon—well chilled—makes a perfect end to an outdoor meal. Melons require no advance preparation, they can be eaten out-of-hand and they are all refreshing. If you like to dress them up a bit, pass port wine and let each guest add a dash to his own serving.

peaches

1. Peel and slice fresh peaches into a large bowl. Sprinkle with maple sugar or brown sugar or add maple syrup to taste. Just before serving, cover with sour cream.

2. Peel and slice fresh peaches into a bowl and sprinkle with sugar. For 6 peaches add ⅓ cup of cognac and let stand for an hour before serving. For frozen peaches, allow about ¼ cup of cognac to a package.

broiled peaches

Either fresh or canned peaches may be broiled (picture, page 112). If fresh, peel the peaches and split in half. Sprinkle them with brown sugar and broil, seed-side-down, for 3 or 4 minutes. Sprinkle the outside with brown sugar, turn and continue broiling 3 to 4 minutes. Place a small dot of butter in the center of each peach half and add a little more brown sugar. Remove to a hot plate and blaze with cognac, if desired. Note: Other fruits, such as pineapple, ripe pears, grapefruit or bananas may be broiled over charcoal or you may combine various fruits on skewers for broiling.

ice cream

America's favorite dessert, ice cream, is always good with an outdoor meal. It combines wonderfully with fresh fruits. Here are some suggestions for ice-cream toppings:

1. Sliced sugared strawberries. Add whipped cream.
2. Crushed sugared raspberries.
3. Blueberries with maple sugar and a little plain sugar added.
4. Sliced sugared peaches with brandy added.
5. Pitted and sugared Bing cherries. Add brandy or kirsch.
6. Sliced sugared nectarines.
7. Sliced sugared apricots.
8. Frozen pineapple or canned crushed pineapple with rum.
9. Any cooked fruit with a heavy syrup or fruit jam or preserve.
10. Cooked gooseberries with plenty of sugar.
11. Sliced and sugared ripe figs.
12. Fresh apricots cooked in a heavy syrup.
13. Wild huckleberries cooked with sugar.

There are also the old standbys, chocolate or butterscotch syrup. Vary them by pouring some maple syrup over ice cream and sprinkling the top with pecans.

COFFEE

■ What wine is to the Frenchman, beer to the German and tea to the Englishman, coffee is to the American. But despite the fact that the coffee maker is used more than any other utensil in the kitchen and on the campfire, its proper use is far too seldom understood.

The brew that you want—a fragrant, clear, flavorful coffee—is simple to achieve regularly if you take care with the procedure each time. In this way, you'll get uniform results—just as a good restaurant does.

First comes the coffee maker. There are dozens of different ones on the market, but they all belong to one of a few basic categories. There is the old-fashioned coffeepot, the percolator and a variety of drip pots and vacuum devices. You'll find them in metal, glass, pottery and porcelain. No matter which you use, the prime secret of making good coffee is to keep the pot clean. Unless your coffee maker is cleaned with soap and water and kept immaculate, you won't get the best results.

Next in importance is the water. Never take water for your coffee from the hot-water tap, or you'll have flat-tasting brew. Use freshly drawn cold water. Especially in the morning, be sure to let the tap run so that you won't use water which has stood overnight in the pipes.

116

If you're camping or picnicking, you'll probably use the old-fashioned pot. Use a full coffee measure or two level tablespoons of coffee for each six-ounce cup of water. To ensure clear coffee by this method I always use a whole egg and shell for six cups. I mix the egg with the coffee and add the cold water. Let the coffee come to the boiling point but don't let it boil. Let it steep for a while. Add a few drops of cold water to settle the grounds. Serve it piping hot.

If you make boiled coffee at home over gas or an electric grill, let it just come to the boil and then add a few drops of cold water. You need not use the egg to settle the grounds where the pot is subjected to less movement during the whole process.

For drip coffee, have a pot that is just large enough for the amount of coffee you want to make (I keep two or three sizes on hand), because you can't make two good cups of coffee in a six-cup pot. Put in a full coffee measure of drip-grind coffee for each six ounces of water. Bring the water to a rolling boil and pour it over the coffee. As soon as the coffee has dripped through, stir it with a spoon. This will ensure your getting an even brew.

There are several different roasts of coffee—the standard American roast, a French roast, which is roasted a bit longer, and the Italian black roast. Contrary to popular belief, there is no chicory in the black-roast coffees. Go to your small coffee dealer and he will show you the different roasts and grind them to your taste. I sometimes mix half French roast and half regular roast for a breakfast coffee, and use the black Italian roast for after-dinner coffee.

Fit your grind to your coffee maker, and if you use different kinds of pots, buy different grinds for them. Freshly ground coffee makes the best brew, and there is an excellent electric grinder on the market which makes short work of turning out the proper amount and grind of coffee for your needs.

I find that ground coffee retains its freshness and flavor best if it's kept in the refrigerator.

All of these points are more important than the type of coffee maker you use. For indoor use, I favor the all-glass drip pot, with paper filters, called Chemex. Any sort of drip pot makes good coffee when kept clean and used at close to its top capacity. If you are careful about timing, a percolator does a good job, too.

iced coffee and tea

These summer beverages are best when made from the freshly brewed product, poured hot over a glass full of ice cubes. Make coffee ⅓ stronger than usual; tea, twice as strong. Float heavy cream on top of your iced coffee if you like a rich drink. Add a sprig of fresh mint to each glass of iced tea—and try a slice of lime as a change from lemon.

When deciding on the cocktails and long drinks you will serve, don't

DRINKS

In this chapter we take it for granted that you don't need to be told to have plenty of iced Cokes or Pepsis, or a large pitcher of fresh-made lemonade, on hand for the small fry at your outdoor party, as well as plenty of cold, cold beer and ale for the grownups to quaff with their food. We assume, too, that if you're serving non-drinkers along with those who like a cocktail or two, you'll provide the former with a tasty fruit- or vegetable-juice substitute. That old standby, tomato juice, can be pepped up considerably by adding a little lemon juice, ½ teaspoon of Worcestershire, salt and pepper to each serving. Tomato juice is also good mixed half-and-half with either sauerkraut juice or clam juice. And as a prelude to an outdoor seafood meal, there's nothing better than a small cup of ice-cold or piping-hot clam juice.

Now for the heartier drinks—the cocktails that sharpen appetites, the long thirst-quenchers for lazy summer days.

COCKTAILS AND LONG DRINKS

■ First, some vodka drinks. This liquor has become increasingly popular during the last few years. It blends well with many other ingredients and has little distinct flavor of its own.

golden screw
For each drink, use 2 ounces of vodka and 3 ounces of orange juice. Shake together with cracked ice. Strain into a chilled glass. This is excellent for Sunday-morning brunch.

hawaiian cooler
For each drink, use 2 ounces of vodka, 2 ounces of pineapple juice and the juice of ½ lime. Shake together with cracked ice and strain into chilled glasses.

bloody mary
This is my favorite. It's a fine pick-up for the morning after, a delight-ful drink before lunch or dinner.

For each drink, use 2 ounces of vodka, 3 ounces of tomato juice, juice

119

of 1 lemon, a dash of Worcestershire sauce, a dash of Tabasco and a pinch of salt. Shake the ingredients together in a shaker with cracked ice. Strain into a large cocktail glass and dust with paprika or celery salt.

martini and gibson

The Martini and the Gibson are good in all seasons of the year, and are probably the most popular American cocktails.

For each drink, use 2 ounces of gin or vodka, ¼ to ½ ounce of dry vermouth and plenty of ice. Stir vigorously with a spoon until thoroughly chilled and blended. Strain into a chilled glass. Add a cocktail onion to each Gibson; a twist of lemon peel or an olive to each Martini.

If you are going out into the country or to the beach to have your outdoor meal, mix your Martinis or Gibsons, chill well and carry them in a thermos jug. Leave in very little, if any, ice—to avoid dilution.

vodka or gin-and-tonic

Summer drinks with quinine water have had quite a vogue lately. I suggest you try several different brands of tonic water to decide which one you like, as they vary considerably in flavor. I prefer Schweppes, because it isn't too sweet. For each drink, use 2 ounces of gin or vodka, cracked ice, a slice of lemon or lime, and tonic water to taste. Pour the gin or vodka into a tall glass filled with cracked ice or ice cubes. Add the slice of lemon or lime and pour in tonic water to taste.

tom collins

The Collins can be made with almost any liquor. Take your pick. For each drink, use 3 ounces of gin, vodka, rum or whisky, juice of 1 lime or 1 lemon, ½ teaspoon of sugar or more, to taste.

Put the ingredients into a shaker with cracked ice and shake vigorously. Pour, ice and all, into a tall chilled glass. Add a splash or so of soda and garnish with a slice of lemon or lime.

whisky sour

For each drink, use 2 ounces of whisky (bourbon, rye or a blend), juice of 1 lemon, sugar to taste (¼ to 1 teaspoon). Put in a shaker with cracked ice and shake well. Strain into a whisky-sour or cocktail glass, add a squirt of soda and a slice of lemon or a half slice of orange.

Make sours of rum, gin or vodka in the same way.

dark rum cocktail

For a large group, use 1 fifth of Jamaica rum, 1 cup of lime juice, ½ cup of honey or maple syrup. Blend these ingredients thoroughly and taste to see if you need any more sweetening or any additional lime juice. Pour into cocktail glasses filled with finely crushed ice.

This cocktail can be made in large quantities ahead of time and kept in a pitcher or jug. Simply pour it into the ice-filled glasses as needed.

planter's punch

For each drink, use 3 ounces of Jamaica rum, 1 ounce of lime juice, 1 teaspoon of sugar or sugar syrup. Pour into a 12-ounce glass filled with ice, add a dash of Angostura bitters and a little plain water to taste.

spritzer

This is a wonderful summer cooler. Simply fill a tall glass with ice, pour in some white wine—preferably a dry white wine—and add a little soda water. Very refreshing.

white wine cassis

Crème de Cassis is a syrup made from black currants and it goes very well in summer drinks. To a good glass of well-chilled white wine add 1 tablespoon Crème de Cassis, or more to taste.

mint julep

There are more versions of this long cold drink than of any other drink I know, and people who are julep fans are apt to be very positive about the superiority of their particular favorite. Here's mine:

For each drink, put about 6 mint leaves in the bottom of a 12-ounce glass or mug. Add 1 teaspoon of sugar (more or less, according to taste) and a dash of branch (tap) water. Use a muddler or spoon and crush the mint against the sides of the glass. Fill the glass to the top with very finely crushed ice, and pour over this 3 ounces of the best bourbon. Stir and stir until the glass begins to frost on the outside. Put it in the refrigerator for a short time, being careful not to rub the frost off with your hands. Just before serving, fill again with crushed ice and add ½ to 1 ounce more of bourbon. Decorate with sprigs of mint dipped in powdered sugar.

fish-house punch

This recipe is for a very large party. It will serve 50 easily. For a smaller group, scale the ingredients down proportionately. Use 2 bottles of Jamaica rum, 1 fifth of cognac, 1 cup of peach or apricot liqueur, 1 quart of tea, 1 quart of lemon juice, 1 quart of water, 1½ cups of granulated sugar or sugar syrup. Let the sugar and lemon juice stand together until the sugar is thoroughly dissolved. Add the other ingredients and let the whole mixture blend in a large punch bowl for 2 hours. About ½ hour before serving add a huge chunk of ice to the bowl and stir well several times.

EQUIPMENT

Many people put a lot of time and money into assembling equipment for outdoor cookery and constructing elaborate outdoor kitchens in their yards or patios. Though this can be fun for the ambitious handyman, it's not necessary. There are many portable grills and braziers on the market that will give you just as tasty a result as the most complicated "made-to-order" job.

If you do have the money, space and desire to build an elaborate outdoor grill with ovens, spits, storage units and accessories, here are a few points to remember:

If you live in a cold climate, lay your foundation below the frost line to prevent cracking and crumbling.

Have electrical outlets placed near your outdoor grill if possible. This enables you to make use of electrical rotisseries, fryers, coffee makers, mixers and many other items that will speed and simplify your cooking.

Make provision for cooking on a spit. This is the most delicious way to cook large cuts of meat and poultry. There are portable spits on the market that can be attached to an outdoor grill in the summer and used indoors in the fireplace in the winter. Some of the new rotisseries are complete portable spitting units in themselves and can be used on the patio, in the kitchen, in the playroom—any place where you have an electrical outlet.

As I've said, it's not necessary to build a complicated outdoor kitchen in order to have delectable feasts. A friend of mine does very well with a unit he built from an old oil can and some discarded grills from a bank teller's window. Many of us have had some of our most memorable meals cooked over an open campfire with a simple grill on top. The portable equipment you can buy today includes everything from the simplest charcoal container up to elaborate pushmobiles that are both glamorous and efficient.

portable grills

There are three different types of portable grill:

1. The Japanese *hibachi,* while a little ponderous to transport in a car, is ideal for small terraces or inside the house itself for grilling steaks, chops and hors d'oeuvres. The most practical of the *hibachi* type of grill is the Skotch Grill, which has proved extremely efficient and can be filled with fuel before setting off on a picnic or cookout.

2. Then there is a small, heavy-duty type of portable grill that comes in a carrying case and can be transported along with its fuel.

3. This past year a new, portable, ceramic-tile grill which burns propane gas has been introduced with great success. This grill, the Bernz-o-matic, comes in several sizes, and it produces—without benefit of charcoal—that much desired charcoal flavor.

wheeled grills

The market for this kind of grill is an ever growing one. Probably the most popular of all of these is a wheeled brazier type of grill which comes in various sizes and at various prices. Some of these brazier types have hoods attached and many have spits. A few are equipped with electrically driven spits. The brazier type that has an adjustable firebox is a most satisfactory unit for most small families, as it does a really efficient grilling job.

The vertical type of grill is usually equipped with two fireboxes and a drip pan underneath. This means that the meat to be grilled is hung between them and cooks on both sides at once. There are many different types of the wheeled flat grill with attached spit unit and hood. Of all these I have found the most consistently efficient unit for either indoors or outdoors is the Bartron barbecue. This stainless-steel stove—for that is what it really is—is so highly perfected that you may install it in the kitchen during the winter months and transfer it to the garden in hot weather. It has two fireboxes, one especially designed for spitting, the other for grilling. The grill is so angled that the fat runs down into a drip pan both when roasting and grilling—a superb example of smart engineering. There is also a multiple-spitted grill for people who enjoy cooking on skewers. Many other types are specially designed to be installed in kitchens or recreation rooms. These are complete with hoods and exhaust fans. Charcoal cookery is not the chore it used to be.

ELECTRIC EQUIPMENT

electric rotisserie

If you do not have an electrically driven spit with your outdoor unit, you may use your household rotisserie—in fact, several of them are much more practical for outdoor use, notably the Town and Country. This is an ideal outdoor unit which can handle a 30-pound turkey, and it has 7 or 8 skewers which will take a variety of meats and fish or a 5- or 6-rib roast of beef. General Electric is manufacturing a new unit of this type which will also accommodate large cuts of meat.

electric skillets and saucepans

Electric skillets have become an invaluable assistant to the outdoor grill. The electric skillet is useful for vegetables, sauces, desserts, casserole dishes and such pleasant outdoor morsels as *sukiyaki*. The electric saucepan which doubles as a French fryer enables you to cook many pleasant accompaniments to your grill on the scene.

SOURCES OF SUPPLY

■ All large department and hardware stores feature the best in bar equipment and accessories. If you want to order by mail, however, you'll find the following list very helpful:

california
BALZER'S, 129 N. Larchmont Blvd., Los Angeles.
VARIOUS BOOTHS IN THE FARMERS' MARKET, W. Third & Fairfax Ave., Los Angeles. Many California roadside stands also sell different types of barbecue equipment.

district of columbia
GAME ROOM, 1538 Connecticut Ave., Washington. Wide range of barbecue, serving and bar accessories.

idaho
WESTERN PRODUCTIONS, 0123 Seventh St., Lewiston. Pioneer Keg Bar, 2½ feet high. $24.95 . . . Other equipment.

illinois
D. CORRADO, INC., 26 N. Clark St., Chicago 2. Butcher block, $6.95 . . . Fine carving cutlery; steak knives, all prices.

VON LENGERKE & ANTOINE, N. Wabash Ave., Chicago. Complete line of accessories.

MARSHALL FIELD & CO., 111 N. State St., Chicago. Complete line of barbecue and bar accessories.

louisiana

SMOKIN' HICKORY HANK, 330 Briar Brae Rd., Lafayette. Bag of hickory-wood disks for $2.95; 3 bags for $7.95.

maryland

"LITTLE JOE" WIESENFELT CO., 112 W. North Ave., Baltimore 1. Bar glasses and mugs, all sizes, prices and designs.

massachusetts

BRECK'S OF BOSTON, Breck Bldg., Boston 10. Complete line of bar accessories.

MASTERCRAFT PRODUCTS, 212 Summer St., Boston 10. Insulated barbecue mitts, $1 pair . . . 5-in-1 gadget, $2.

CORCORAN, INC., Stoughton. Outdoor grill of heavy-gauge metal, welded-wire grid; folds to 14"x18" unit in carrying case, $6.45 . . . Other cooking, serving and outing equipment.

minnesota

MILMARS, P.O. Box 722, Minneapolis. Chef-Master indoor-outdoor broiler, steel, 14"x18" grill, $12.95.

GOKEY CO., 94 E. Fourth St., St. Paul 1. Portable cooler, Fiberglas insulation, 19"x12"x10", $14.95 . . . Butcher's wood block, $4.95 . . . Many other useful items.

new jersey

BUYWAYS, P.O. Box 224, Orange. Old-fashioned coffeepot, holds 35 cups, $4.95. Other utensils and implements.

DOROTHY DAMAR, Damar Bldg., Newark 5. Ice crusher, $1.98 . . . Ten-ounce thermo tumblers, 4 for $3.98 . . . Gay Nineties jigger glasses, 8 for $1.50 . . . Other equipment.

new york

ABERCROMBIE & FITCH, 45th St. & Madison Ave., N.Y.C. Complete assortment of barbecue and camp-cooking accessories.

BAR MART, 62 W. 45th St., N.Y.C. Wide assortment of barbecue aids includes outdoor-chef apron sets, asbestos gloves, Big Boy braziers and folding aluminum tables . . . Full line of bar accessories.

HAMMACHER SCHLEMMER, 145 E. 57th St., N.Y.C. Carving platter with meat holder; solid maple, 18"x12", well and tree design, $9.95 . . .

Big Boy rotisseries, barbecue grills and braziers range up to $300.00. Many, many accessories.

HOFFRITZ FOR CUTLERY, 49 E. 34th St., N.Y.C. Full line of cutlery, serving and bar accessories.

BAZAR FRANCAIS, 666 Sixth Ave., N.Y.C. Cooking and serving gear; warmers, soup servers, roll heaters, French copper utensils, pepper mills, bread baskets, coffee makers, etc.

DAVID T. ABERCROMBIE, 97 Chambers St., N.Y.C. Wide range of outdoor cooking equipment.

LA CUISINIERE, 133 E. 55th St., N.Y.C. Fine knives, utensils, exceptionally good imported omelet pan and skillet in cast aluminum.

wisconsin

HOUSE OF IDEAS, 1309 State St., Racine. Butcher block, $5.95. Kebab skewers, 28 inches, 6 for $3.95.

MILES KIMBALL, Kimball Bldg., Oshkosh. Thermobag, keeps contents hot or cold 6 to 8 hours, holds 16 to 18 bottles, $5.95. Many other accessories and utensils.

FOODS AND SEASONINGS

california

BALZER'S, 129 N. Larchmont Blvd., Los Angeles. Practically everything in the line of fine foods—cheese, herbs, preserved fish, etc.

FARMERS' MARKET, W. Third & Fairfax Ave., Los Angeles. Write for a list of dealers in the market who mail-order every type of foreign and domestic food.

GOLDBERG BOWEN, 242 Sutter St., San Francisco. Virtually everything in food, including Chinese and Mexican specialties.

JURGENSEN'S, 842 E. California, Pasadena.

georgia

RICH'S, INC., 45 Broad St., S.W., Atlanta. Fine assortment of domestic and imported delicacies.

illinois

MARSHALL FIELD & CO., 111 N. State St., Chicago. A choice assortment of fancy groceries and imported specialties.

STOP AND SHOP, 16 W. Washington St., Chicago. Practically everything in food and equipment.

louisiana

A. M. & J. SOLARI, 201 Royal St., New Orleans. One of the greatest food shops in the South.

maine

MAINE FRESH LOBSTER COMPANY, Rockport. Various combinations of live lobsters and clams, shipped anywhere within 2,000 miles, packed in seaweed and ready to cook in the tin they're shipped in.

massachusetts

S. S. PIERCE & CO., 133 Brookline Ave., Boston. The country's oldest dealer in fine foods. Pierce will send anything in the way of groceries by mail to any point in the U.S.

missouri

WOLFERMAN'S, 120 W. 47th St., Kansas City. This shop carries an excellent line of food products.

new york

J. & J. W. ELSWORTH CO., Greenport, Long Island. Oysters in the shell or opened, packed in ice and guaranteed to arrive fresh and alive anywhere in the U.S.

THE FORSTS, Route 297, Kingston. Smoked turkeys, $1.70 per pound. Many other delicacies.

BLOOMINGDALE'S DELICACY SHOP, Lexington Ave. & 59th St., N.Y.C. All types of food. Perishables are sent by Air Express.

B. ALTMAN & CO., 34th St. & Fifth Ave., N.Y.C. All types of imported and domestic foods.

SOUPCON, 205 E. 61st St., N.Y.C. Fine French foods, dressings and sauces; French cooking utensils.

TRINACRIA DELICATESSEN, 29th St. & Third Ave., N.Y.C. Italian pastas, seasonings, beans, dry vegetables; utensils.

WING FAT & CO., 34 Mott St., N.Y.C. All Chinese specialties. Fresh vegetables sent Air Express at extra cost.

CASA MONEO, 218 W. 14th St., N.Y.C. Every Mexican and Spanish specialty, fine oils and wine vinegars; utensils.

KATAGIRI & CO., 224 E. 58th St., N.Y.C. Japanese specialties.

ORIENTAL FOOD SHOP, 2791 Broadway, N.Y.C. Everything in imported and domestic Japanese provisions.

oregon

MEIER & FRANK CO., Portland. This old department store has almost every food specialty.

texas

ASHLEY'S, INC., P.O. Box 3040, Station A, El Paso. This large shop packs all the Mexican specialties. Order directly, or write for the names of stores near you that carry Ashley's brand.